Berlitz

KUALA LUMPUR

POCKET GUIDE

G000241026

201848051

Walking Eye
mobile app

Discover the world's best destinations with the Insight Guides Walking Eye app, available to download for free in the App Store and Google Play.

The container app provides easy access to fantastic free content on events and activities taking place in your destination, with the possibility of booking, up-to-the-minute hotel and travel details, an A to Z of practical information and Insight Guides' pick of what to see and do to inspire you. The app also allows you to download Insight Guides, with the option to purchase and download other destination guides through the app.

WEST SUSSEX LIBRARY SERVICE

201848051	
Askews & Holts	19-Feb-2019
915.951	

INSIGHT GUIDES

Walking Eye

⊙ **DESTINATIONS**

⊘ **INSPIRE ME**

▱ **EBOOKS**

▦ **EVENTS**

TOP 10 ATTRACTIONS

KUALA GANDAH ELEPHANT CONSERVATION CENTRE
A chance to observe and learn about Asian elephants. See page 80.

NIGHTSPOTS
From sophisticated bars to hot clubs, KL offers great nightlife options. See page 89.

COLONIAL CORE
Majestic Mughal-style architecture of the late 19th century. See page 29.

BATU CAVES
A beautiful limestone cave temple with Hindu shrines and statues. See page 76.

CENTRAL MARKET
Home to lively art and craft shops. See page 33.

SIN SZE SI YA TEMPLE
An important Taoist temple that honours early leader Yap Ah Loy. See page 35.

ISLAMIC ARTS MUSEUM MALAYSIA
Artefacts from the Muslim world displayed in a graceful building. See page 53.

RUMAH PENGHULU ABU SEMAN
A rare ancient Malay timber house in modern KL. See page 74.

PETRONAS TWIN TOWERS
These skyscrapers, among the world's tallest, are stunning both day and night. See page 60.

CANOPY WALKWAY
Walk among the tree tops at the Forest Research Institute of Malaysia. See page 79.

A PERFECT DAY

8.00am

Hainanese breakfast

Enjoy a breakfast of toast with coconut jam and local tea or coffee at the Cafe Old Market Square traditional Hainanese coffee shop in Medan Pasar Lama (see page 107). Note the magnificent Dutch gables on the row of pre-war shophouses in which it sits.

10.00am

A bit of culture

Walk to Jalan Tun H.S. Lee and explore the temples here, including the Taoist Sin Sze Si Ya temple honouring one of the city fathers and the Hindu Sri Maha Mariamman temple. Soak up the atmosphere of Petaling Street and its surrounds.

1.00pm

Nonya lunch

Take a lunch break and respite from the heat at the Old China Café Nonya restaurant on Jalan Balai Polis. Then head south to see the Chan She Shu Yuen Clan Association Building and, if you have time, the Guan Yin temple before getting on the monorail at the Maharajalela station.

8.30am

Colonial core

Stroll over to the confluence of the rivers Klang and Gombak, where the city began, and then to Dataran Merdeka to take in the Moghul architecture of the colonial core. There is an excellent model of the area in the Kuala Lumpur City Gallery.

IN KUALA LUMPUR

5.00pm

Towers galore

Walk or take a taxi to the KL Tower (Menara Kuala Lumpur), where you can get a great bird's-eye view of the city, including the country's tallest buildings, the Petronas Twin Towers.

2.30pm

Malay heritage

The monorail goes through the frenetic shopping area of Bukit Bintang. Get off at the Raja Chulan stop and head to the Badan Warisan Malaysia (Heritage of Malaysia Trust) to take the 3pm tour of the beautiful Rumah Penghulu Abu Seman traditional Malay house (book beforehand, closed on Sun).

7.00pm

Cocktails at sunset

Head downhill and across Jalan Punchak to the Pacific Regency Hotel Suites, where you can relax at the ultra-chic Luna on the 34th floor, sipping a cocktail while watching the city lights come on from this spectacular viewpoint.

8.30pm

Fusion fare

If you are hungry, head round the corner to Elegant Inn at Menara Hap Seng (see page 110) for creative Cantonese fare, including the outstanding dim sum the place is famous for, or Cuisine Gourmet by Nathalie at Menara Taipan (see page 109) for contemporary French food.

10.30pm

All-night clubbing

From here, walk along Jalan P. Ramlee till you hit the big clubs like the Beach Club Café and Poppy Collection. There is more swanky action at the Asian Heritage Row on Jalan Dang Wangi. For live jazz and pubs, head instead to Changkat Bukit Bintang.

CONTENTS

INTRODUCTION

Kuala Lumpur – or KL, as it is fondly called – is proudly progressive and cosmopolitan, with aspirations to achieve 'world-class city' status. The trademarks of this ambition include an ever-changing skyscraper skyline, the conspicuous presence of global brand names and an educated populace as well versed in English Premier League politics as in China's superpower status. However, visitors to KL are likely to be impressed most with its multi-ethnic Asian rhythms, colour and bustle. From myriad cultural and religious sites and festivals, to a mouth-wateringly large

⊙ THE MALAYS

Originally from southern China and Taiwan, Malays (the *Melayu* people) arrived in the Malay Archipelago 3,000–5,000 years ago. Through the years, they intermarried and assimilated with other Chinese, Indians, Arabs and Thais. Malaysia's Federal Constitution defines a Malay as one who practises Islam and Malay culture, speaks the Malay language, and whose ancestors are Malays. Malay culture shows strong Javanese, Sumatran, Siamese and especially Indian influence. Linguistically, Malay is Austronesian, but people will recognise vocabulary that is Arabic, Sanskrit, Tamil, Portuguese, Dutch, Chinese and English.

Malays are also grouped officially as *bumiputra*, literally 'sons of the soil'. This political term was coined to ensure Malays' constitutional 'special position', the basis for indigeneity and hence special rights. *Bumiputra* also encompasses the indigenous people of the peninsula, Sabah and Sarawak, as well as Indian Muslims and Thai and Portuguese Malaysians.

choice of food, the multi-faceted threads of Malay, Chinese, Indian and other Asian traditions and sensibilities are intricately woven into the fabric of this city.

A CAPITAL CITY

Kuala Lumpur is the capital of Malaysia, which comprises Peninsular Malaysia and the states of Sabah and Sarawak on the island of Borneo. Located midway down the peninsula's west coast, KL has

New Year lanterns and signage on Chinatown's Petaling Street

an area of 234 sq km (90 sq miles). It anchors Klang Valley, the country's most developed and prosperous conurbation, which spreads over 1,600 sq km (618 sq miles) and has a population of 6.84 million, about a third of whom work in KL. Annexed from the state of Selangor, KL is one of the country's three Federal Territories and the seat of Parliament. The administrative and judicial capital is Putrajaya in the south.

The city's oldest sections date back 150 years, but much of the city was modernised in the 1990s, when the country experienced double-digit Gross Domestic Product growth, fuelling a property and infrastructure boom. Density has increased, many old neighbourhoods have been redeveloped, and postmodern architecture dominates the cityscape. Visitors are often surprised at how green KL is, with parks and gardens within the city and lush rainforests on its outskirts. The latter make up the natural tropical forests that cover about 40 percent of Malaysia.

AN ECONOMIC MAGNET

The indigenous Orang Asli people are believed to have been the first inhabitants of the area, but they have long been relegated to the city's fringes. Many of today's KL-ites have their roots elsewhere in the country. A large number of people relocated to KL in the 1960s, when the country's economy shifted from an agricultural to industrial base. They were drawn by jobs and good facilities, and now enjoy the country's highest per capita GDP and best employment rates. This is why KL continues to attract youngsters from all over Malaysia, as well as migrant workers from other countries, upon whom the city's economy heavily relies.

MULTIPLE CULTURES

Ethnically, KL's 2 million inhabitants are made up of a majority of Chinese and Malays and a minority of Indians. However, these simplistic categories cannot encapsulate the rainbow of peoples that make up a social landscape that goes back to the beginning of trade in the Malay Peninsula in 200BC. Over the centuries, assimilations and adaptations have been motley, creative and widespread in everything from language to architecture, fashion to social mores. The contemporary influences of education, affluence and globalisation continue to iron out ethnic differences.

Nonetheless, core ethnic values are retained, especially when it comes to religion. The Chinese are largely Buddhists, Taoists or

Malaysian English

KL-ites use a wide variety of English, from East-Coast American to Received Pronunciation, and versions infused with vocabulary from any or all of the local languages. What is evident is that KL-ites love their 'Englishes' and have fun with them.

Christian, the Malays are Muslim and the Indians Hindu, Muslim or Christian. Other faiths practised include Sikhism and Bahai. Constitutionally, Islam is the official religion, but freedom of religion is generally guaranteed, as is evident in the coexistence of different places of worship and religious celebrations throughout the city.

Traditional musicians

TOURIST-FRIENDLY

As the country's financial and commercial centre, Kuala Lumpur has a large number of global service centres for accountancy, advertising, banking and law. The city is leading national efforts towards developing a services-based economy, one of the city's key income-earners being tourism. As such, KL is tourist-oriented, offering easily available tourist information and clear signposts to key attractions. The hospitality industry is well organised and largely English-speaking. However, service standards might not be up to par in some hotels and restaurants, particularly with the dependence on migrant workers whom local bosses have not trained properly.

As KL grew city planners neglected to make it pedestrian- or disabled-friendly. A saving grace is the existence of good rail systems, which are the only way to get around during the badly gridlocked 8–9.30am and 5–7pm rush hours. Taxis are plentiful, but their drivers have a nasty reputation for charging exorbitant fees during peak hours and after midnight.

The Petronas Twin Towers

ORIENTATION

Navigating the city is fairly easy. Road signs can sometimes be confusing, but friendly KL-ites are at hand to help with directions.

The city basically has two centres. The old city centre is at the confluence of the rivers Klang and Gombak. West of the confluence is the colonial core, where 19th-century British rulers built their administrative buildings. Southeast of the confluence is the mainly Chinese enclave around Petaling Street, now the site of the city's liveliest night market. North of the confluence is Masjid India, a mainly Indian Muslim area, and north of that, Kampung Baru, the oldest Malay settlement in KL.

The new city centre, called the Kuala Lumpur City Centre (KLCC), is located northeast of the historic part of town and anchors the commercial and business district. KLCC is home to the Petronas Twin Towers, among the tallest buildings in the world. South of this are Bukit Bintang – which packs more shops, hotels and restaurants per square kilometre than anywhere else in the country – and the nightlife magnets of the swanky Asian Heritage Row, Jalan P. Ramlee and Changkat Bukit Bintang.

Outside the city, nature-lovers may enjoy the Forest Research Institute of Malaysia, Kuala Gandah Elephant Conservation Centre and the cool highland retreat of Fraser's Hill. Las Vegas types should head to Genting Highlands for its casino and theme parks.

A BRIEF HISTORY

Lush lowland tropical rainforest originally covered the Malay Peninsula, which was peopled first by small numbers of indigenous Orang Asli. When Malays and other peoples started settling in the peninsula, the Orang Asli were pushed inland to areas where forests still existed. However, they remained key to the sourcing of natural forest products for trade. When tin was discovered, towns began to spring up and the Orang Asli were further marginalised.

THE SEARCH FOR TIN

By the middle of the 19th century the Malay Peninsula was an ethnically diverse land of plenty, as well as an international trading centre for tin, spices and other natural resources. Locally, this trade was controlled by Malay sultans such as Selangor's Raja Abdullah. Raja Abdullah was based in the area's capital town of Klang, where he could tax goods and produce that came down the main transport artery of the Klang river. He left the running of the area's tin mines to his Chinese managers, who had access to thousands of indentured labourers escaping poverty in China.

It was in search of tin that, in 1857, at the behest of their Malay royal master, 87 Chinese coolies rowed up the Klang river. When they came to a confluence and the waters became too shallow, they continued inland on foot through swamps and hostile jungle. Luckily, they were rewarded with the discovery of tin. Unluckily, all of them soon died of malaria. However, they did manage to set up a camp at their disembarkation point, the confluence of the Klang and Gombak rivers. This place was called Kuala Lumpur, literally Muddy Estuary. That this would one day be a capital city with global aspirations would have been beyond anyone's imagining.

YAP AH LOY TAKES CONTROL

Kuala Lumpur became another typical mining town, dominated by the Chinese and characterised by wooden shanties, squalor, iniquity and fierce rivalries between secret societies. Activities centred on the eastern river bank of the confluence at Market Square, an area now called Medan Pasar Lama. The rabble was led by community leaders called *Kapitan Cina* (literally 'Chinese Captain'), who were largely ineffectual in imposing order until Yap Ah Loy, the third *Kapitan Cina*, took over in 1868. A feared

⊙ THE GREAT TRADING PAST

Thanks to its fortuitous location between two major sea routes and monsoonal wind systems, the Malay Peninsula has been at the heart of international trade for thousands of years. The trade centred on the Malay Archipelago's rich natural resources, particularly spices, which in the peninsula were harvested by the indigenous Orang Asli, who brought these products to the coasts and exchanged them with the Malays. They in turn traded them with merchants from the rest of the archipelago, India and China, with whom trading links go back to 200BC.

By the time the great trading empire of Malacca reached its apex in the 15th century, Chinese, Indians, Persians, Arabs and Malays from the rest of the archipelago (now Indonesia) had forged long-standing business and cultural relationships with the locals and each other, established settlements in the peninsula and brought influences that ranged from religion and language to food.

Control of this trade was what attracted the colonising powers from Portugal, then Holland, and finally Britain from the 15th century onwards.

and respected gang leader who was also a relentless peacekeeper, Yap was police chief, judge, tax collector and property developer as well as a brothel and opium-den operator. His tenacity and enterprise were what prevented Kuala Lumpur from disappearing back into the jungle. During his two-decade tenure, he rebuilt the settlement three times, after the Selangor Civil War, a massive fire and an enormous flood.

Yap Ah Loy

It was the Civil War (1867–73) that led to British interference in Selangor and Kuala Lumpur. The British had established themselves in the Straits Settlements of Penang, Malacca and Singapore and controlled the maritime trading routes. However, they left local affairs outside these areas to the sultans. As world demand for tin escalated due to the growth of the canning industry, Selangor's local chieftains became more powerful and started fighting over political authority and taxation. Forming alliances became an integral strategy in their warmongering.

Raja Abdullah died, but the faction belonging to his son eventually gained control of Selangor through an ally, Tengku Kudin. Tengku Kudin sought and received the support of Yap Ah Loy. He also borrowed war funds from merchants in Malacca and Singapore and got armed assistance from British authorities. However, merchants and administrators had started to become concerned about their investments and trade stability in Selangor.

BRITISH RULE

In 1876, the British installed a Resident in Selangor to extend to the Malay ruler the 'protection' of the British Empire. The Resident's role was basically to ensure that trade would flourish by imposing British regulations and systems.

By 1880, Selangor's capital had been moved from Klang to Kuala Lumpur. Two years later, under British Resident Frank Swettenham, the modernisation of Kuala Lumpur began, using funds mobilised once again by Yap Ah Loy. Finally, the wooden shanties were replaced by brick buildings, laterite roads were built to the mining areas, and a railway line constructed that linked Kuala Lumpur to Klang. A Sanitary Board was also established to provide town council services.

KL was a bustling little town at that time. A Malay and Indian Muslim enclave had sprung up north of the river confluence in an area now called Jalan Masjid India. Many of these early settlers were traders and miners of Sumatran, Bugis, Rawa and Mandailing origins, broadly referred to as Malays. Indian Muslim traders also set up shop here. Their wares were textiles and other products from the Indian subcontinent; items long traded in this land. This area north of the confluence also became the main shopping strip for the British colonials.

The main Chinese communities lived east of the confluence, in the enclave around Jalan Petaling, and comprised Hakka and Cantonese peoples. As KL prospered, they came to dominate business and commerce and make up the majority of the town's population. The European quarter was west of the confluence on the hills overlooking the Lake Gardens.

A COLONIAL CAPITAL

In 1896, the British formed the Federated Malay States (FMS) to centralise administration and fast-track economic

Frank Swettenham's residence, now the Carcosa Hotel

development. By this time, the peninsula was producing more than half the world's tin. KL became the FMS capital and Swettenham its first Resident-General. The town now had to live up to its new status of colonial capital, as well as inspire the confidence of investors. Therefore, a new government administrative core was constructed, designed to be suitably imposing yet also reflect the Islamic mores of the land. Colonial town-planners chose to adapt their version of the Mughal architectural style of North India. The administrative core centred on the monumental Sultan Abdul Samad Building, which remained the heart of KL for well over a century.

Unlike the Chinese, few Malays wanted to relocate to Kuala Lumpur. The British plan was to groom a small, elite group of Malays to participate in local administration. To attract them, the colonials established Kampung Baru (literally 'New Village'), north of the confluence, which today remains

A post-war image of the Sultan Abdul Samad Building

almost exclusively Malay. British-educated civil servants from South India were brought to Malaya to fill government positions in the railways, plantations and other clerical services. Labourers were also brought in to build the railways. Government quarters were provided for local civil servants in Brickfields, southeast of the city, where bricks were once manufactured to rebuild early KL. Later, railway-marshalling yards were located on the northern side of Brickfields. This is now the city's rail transport hub.

By the turn of the century, another economic product, one introduced by the British, took root in Malaya: rubber. Fuelled by the rubber-tyre boom, thousands of hectares of jungle were converted to plantations, and by 1916 rubber surpassed tin as Malaya's main export. Planters started flooding KL's colonial hang-outs. An influx of indentured labour from India changed the social landscape of Malaya again. The British administered what had become a complex plural society as three crude and ill-defined groups: Malays, Chinese and Indians, each identified with specific economic roles to serve the goal of developing the colonial economy.

When World War II hit Malaya in 1941, the British were ill-prepared to defend the Malay Peninsula and fled, allowing the Japanese an easy takeover. Ruling with an iron fist, the

Japanese singled out the Chinese for brutalisation. This gave rise to a local, largely Chinese-based communist movement that engaged the Japanese in guerrilla warfare. At the same time, the Japanese encouraged incipient Malay nationalism.

TOWARDS INDEPENDENCE

In 1945, the Japanese surrendered and the British returned to Malaya with a centralised administration plan to recover lost economic ground, but with the aim of paving the way for self-rule. They proposed a united nation with equal rights for all ethnic communities. However, the leaders of a rising brand of Malay nationalistic politics rejected the proposal in favour of a federation recognising the sovereignty of the sultans, the individuality of the states and Malay privileges. At the forefront of this nationalism was the United Malays National Organization (UMNO), the Malay-based political party that continued to dominate politics in modern Malaysia until 2018.

Meanwhile, finding themselves shut out of public life, the communists decided that only armed struggle would lead to independence, which led the British to declare a state of emergency in 1948. The 'Emergency' was to last until 1960.

During this time, UMNO joined forces with two other ethnic-based political parties, the Malaysian Chinese Association (MCA) and Malaysian Indian Congress (MIC) to seek an independence acceptable to the British. After winning the first Malayan election, the alliance formed the government of the Federation of Malaya under Prime Minister Tunku Abdul Rahman in 1957, uniting all the peninsular states. Kuala Lumpur was retained as the capital. Six years later, the British colonies of Singapore, Sabah and Sarawak joined Malaya to form Malaysia, although Singapore withdrew two years later.

The National Monument

SHAPING A MODERN MALAYSIA

Colonial-era inequalities among Malaysians were not addressed fully at Malaysia's independence, and language and education soon became key issues of contention. In 1969, emotionally charged elections saw a shocking erosion of the traditional majority support for the ruling alliance (now the National Front) in favour of two Chinese opposition parties. Immediately after, politically engineered, bloody clashes occurred between Malays and Chinese on 13 May in Kampung Baru and Chow Kit. The violence lasted just four days but had a long-term effect on the political landscape of Malaysia, resulting in the imposition of the controversial New Economic Policy (NEP).

Massive industrialisation in the 1970s saw the migration of rural populations, particularly Malays, to urban areas, including Kuala Lumpur. In 1974, KL became a Federal Territory administered by the Kuala Lumpur City Hall. Skyscrapers sprung up, and, to ease overcrowding in KL, vast housing estates were built in the surrounding areas.

During the 'Asian Tiger' economic boom decade of the 1990s, the Klang Valley – and KL in particular – saw intense construction and mega projects. These were driven by the charismatic Prime Minister Dr Mahathir Mohamad (first term: 1981–2003), whom critics decried for authoritarian rule, which they claimed included muzzling the media, judiciary and royalty, and establishing economic policies that bred cronyism and corruption. Despite this, he put KL on the world map by building the Petronas Twin Towers in the new Kuala Lumpur City Centre, developing the Silicon Valley-type Multimedia Super Corridor, and creating a brand-new federal capital at Putrajaya.

THE RISE OF PEOPLE POWER

The good times ended with the Asian Economic Crisis in 1997. The following year, the arrest of former Deputy Prime Minister Anwar Ibrahim on corruption and sodomy charges, after he had tried to tackle issues of corruption within UMNO and the coalition, sparked a massive anti-government demonstration. Nonetheless, Mahathir had reined in both economic and social chaos by the time he stepped down. However, a growing number of Malaysians were now voicing dissatisfaction over issues such as abuse of the NEP and power by politicos and their business allies, as well as

New Economic Policy

The New Economic Policy (NEP) aimed to address ethnic and economic inequality and to eradicate poverty by growing the economic pie. In 1970, 75 percent of Malaysians living below the poverty line were Malay, and so affirmative action for the bumiputra (which include Malays; see page 10) became part of institutional life.

Malay women shopping

judicial corruption and the lack of religious freedom.

Protest votes in the 2008 elections cost the National Front its biggest ever number of seats, surprising the entire nation in the beginnings of a tsunami of change. Along with five other states, KL-ites voted in a majority of opposition Members of Parliament. Importantly, the electorate now realised they had the power to change government.

Despite attempts to quell fears of electoral fraud, to convince Malaysians that unity was a governmental priority, and to assert that corruption was being addressed, the issues bubbled up again in a highly contentious run-up to the 2018 general election. Embroiled in fresh corruption allegations, incumbent Prime Minister Najib Razak faced off against his party's former leader, Dr Mahathir Mohamad, who now fronted a rival coalition, Pakatan Harapan (the Alliance of Hope).

Now aged 92, Mahathir's victory came as a shock. One key aspect of his win was a promise to end the kind of political corruption over which he himself had once presided during his first term. In another surprising turn, Mahathir announced that his former enemy, Anwar Ibrahim, would succeed him as Prime Minister after a few years. Ibrahim received a full royal pardon, after decades of intermittent imprisonment and trials. The stage has finally been set to give the Malaysian people a cleaner government.

HISTORICAL LANDMARKS

74,000BC Ancestors of indigenous people settle in the Malay Peninsula.

200BC China and India begin trading with the Malay Archipelago.

AD700 The region comes under Hindu-Buddhist influences.

1300s The region comes under Islamic influences.

1511 The era of colonisation begins.

1857 Kuala Lumpur becomes a staging point for tin.

1868 Yap Ah Loy becomes *Kapitan Cina* and brings order to the town.

1874 British colonialism in the Malay Peninsula begins.

1880 KL declared Selangor's capital.

1882 Beginning of KL's modernisation by Frank Swettenham and Yap Ah Loy.

1896 Formation of the Federated Malay States under British rule.

1930s Rise of nationalism among Malays and anti-colonialism among communist Chinese.

1941–5 Japanese occupation.

1948–60 State of Emergency; counter-insurgency against communists.

1955 Malaya's first national election held; the Alliance of ethnic-based political parties wins 80 percent of votes.

1957 On 31 August, Malaya is proclaimed independent, with KL as capital. Architectural icons of statehood built in KL.

1963 Malaysia is formed, comprising Peninsular Malaysia, Singapore, Sabah and Sarawak; Singapore withdraws in 1965.

1970 Nationwide New Economic Policy is introduced.

1974 KL is annexed from Selangor to become a Federal Territory.

1988–97 Skyscrapers transform KL's cityscape during tiger economy period of 9 percent per annum GDP growth; ended by the Asian Economic Crisis.

2008 Malaysia's 12th general election results in unexpected and historic losses by the ruling political coalition.

2012 Largest-ever street demonstration demanding electoral reform; general election.

2016 Muhammad V replaces Abdul Halim Mu'adzam Shah as sultan.

2018 Dr Mahathir Mohamad is elected as prime minister for the second time at the age of 92 in the 14th general election as leader of the BERSATU party.

The colonial Sultan Abdul Samad building

WHERE TO GO

Explore Kuala Lumpur's old city centre first before moving on to the new city centre, then out to its green and rural outskirts. The city wears different faces in the day and at night, making some sites worth revisiting later. KL assumes a different aura again during festivities, particularly in the relevant ethnic hubs, such as Petaling Street and Bukit Bintang during Chinese New Year and Kampung Baru during the Muslim Hari Raya Puasa. To make the most of your visit, feel free to wander off and check out nooks and corners that seem interesting, though this is not always a good idea at night. Many famous sights are featured in guided bus tours, but it is often best to use trains or walk whenever possible to avoid the traffic jams.

AROUND DATARAN MERDEKA

Despite being almost smothered by tall buildings and elevated rail tracks, the historic river confluence where Kuala Lumpur was born remains intact, a tribute to the city's origins. West of the confluence is the colonial core, a collection of British-Mughal-style administrative buildings standing around the Dataran Merdeka square. Towering above them is a giant flag-pole, proclamation of the country's independence.

OLD MARKET SQUARE

The **Old Market Square** ❶ (Medan Pasar Lama) is where the city's first brick buildings were erected in the 1880s. Bordered by Lebuh Pasar Besar and Medan Pasar, the square now hosts a busy bus stop and a clock tower, built in 1937 to

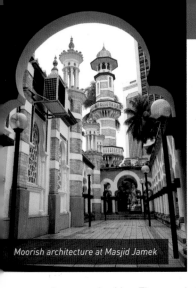
Moorish architecture at Masjid Jamek

commemorate the coronation of England's King George VI. A wet-produce market once occupied this square, but in 1936 it was relocated about 1km (0.6 miles) south to Central Market (see page 33), which is now a souvenir and arts complex.

Overlooking the square are several handsome triple-storey Chinese shophouses from the early 20th century, with neoclassical features such as columns and gables. These period shophouses are still found all over the old heart of KL and were used by families both as a home (upstairs) and to conduct business (downstairs). The shophouses are connected by continuous pedestrian verandas called five-foot ways, which really are 5ft (1.5m) wide. They originated in Singapore in 1822, the invention of colonial administrator Stamford Raffles, who deemed them essential for providing reprieve from the weather.

North of this square on Jalan Benteng you can get an excellent view of the historic confluence of the rivers Klang and Gombak. The triangular piece of land at the confluence is occupied by the graceful **Masjid Jamek** ❷ (Jamek Mosque; Sat–Thu 8.30am–12.30pm, 2.30–4.15pm and 5.30–6.30pm, Fri 8.30–10.30am, 2.30–4.15pm and 5.30–6.30pm), a sprawl of colonnades and minarets. Built in 1909 in the British-Mughal style, this is the city's oldest mosque.

THE COLONIAL CORE

The colonial core spreads west of the confluence, girdled by Jalan Raja. This area was the civic heart of the Federated Malay States (FMS) and, later, the Federation of Malaya, from the late 19th century until 1957, when the country gained independence from the British. The colonial architects created an institutional architectural style for the capital that combined Western neo-classical and decorative Islamic Mughal features imported from their Indian outpost. The buildings are heavily symmetrical yet feature the liberal use of domes, arches and minarets. After independence, most of these edifices served as courts before they were taken over by government departments.

At the corner of Jalan Tun Perak and Jalan Raja is a trio of buildings. The first is the former **FMS Survey Office**, which was constructed in 1910 and sports black domes and clover-leafed arches. Adjoining it is the **Old Town Hall**, differenti-ated from the former by a stepped pediment. Both of these buildings have domed porches. Behind it, shaped like a wide 'V', is the **Old High Court**, distinguished by pepper-pot turrets and double-columned arches.

The Gombak river sepa-rates these buildings from the pièce de résistance of the colonial core, the **Sultan Abdul Samad Building** ❸ (Bangunan Sultan Abdul Samad). Stretching 137m (450ft) along Jalan Raja and

Saturday nightlife

Jalan Raja is frequently closed to traffic on Satur-day nights when events are held at the Padang. The area then becomes a hang-out for families, youngsters and tourists taking in the bright lights illuminat-ing the colonial core. The boulevard is also the venue for the colourful cultural parade that opens the Col-ours of Malaysia (Citra-warna) tourism event.

In the streets around the colonial core

anchored by a square clock tower, this vision of columns and arches was the city's first Mughal-style building. When it officially opened in 1897, KL had never seen anything like it. It served as offices for the FMS Secretariat and a host of other departments.

A lane separates the Sultan Abdul Samad Building from the **Old General Post Office**, though the two are linked by an arched bridge. The post office is distinguished by pointed arches, leaf-shaped pediments and rooftop pinnacles.

Next to this building, on the other side of the arched bridge, is the **Straits Trading Building**, which has been modernised and now houses the Industrial Court (Mahkamah Perusahaan). The court also occupies the historical building next to it, a corner pink-and-white edifice that once housed KL's first department store, **Chow Kit & Co**. The store was established in the 1890s by a KL millionaire to cater to colonials, and this site was chosen because it was close to the Klang river, where supplies could easily be unloaded.

The last Mughal-style building on this side of Jalan Raja is on the other side of Jalan Medan Pasar. The orange-and-white banded building is a showcase of ornamental rectangular columns and brick. It was originally the colonial **FMS Railway Headquarters**. It now houses the **National Textile Museum**

(Muzium Tekstil Negara; www.muziumtekstilnegara.gov.my; daily 9am–6pm), whose displays comprise historical textiles and ornaments of the different ethnic groups. It has a lovely café and gift shop.

DATARAN MERDEKA

Opposite the Sultan Abdul Samad Building is a field of green anchored at the far end by a massive flagpole. This is **Dataran Merdeka** (literally Independence Square), originally a sports field that also served as the British parade grounds. Here, on 31 August 1957, the Union flag was lowered and the new Malayan flag raised at midnight to the chimes of the clock on the Sultan Abdul Samad Building. Since independence, Dataran Merdeka has become the venue of the annual countdown to National Day (Hari Kemerdekaan), as well as New Year's Day.

On the other side of the square, facing the Sultan Abdul Samad Building, are several mock-Tudor buildings. They make up the **Royal Selangor Club** (Kelab Diraja Selangor), a members-only social club frequented by high society. In colonial times, administrators, planters, merchants and their wives would gather here for a *setengah* (whisky soda) and to catch up on gossip. Although the club was founded in 1884, the current building dates back only to 1978, when it was rebuilt after a fire.

To the right of the Club, hidden by trees, is one of the region's oldest Anglican churches, **St Mary's Cathedral** (Jalan Raja; www.stmaryscathedral.org.my; open daily for worshippers). Built in the English Gothic style, it was consecrated in 1887 and became the main place of worship for the English. The current building was constructed in 1922, following a fire, and features stained-glass windows that honour colonial planters and depict tropical crops such as rubber and palm oil.

At the southern end of Dataran Merdeka, on the other side of Lebuh Pasar, is the old **Chartered Bank of India, Australia and China**, with whom the colonial government held all its accounts. This 1891 three-storey period piece is bedecked with domes and arcades.

The building on its west side is the former **Government Printing Office**, which was built around the same period as the rest of the colonial core, but sports a relatively simple neo-Renaissance design that breaks with the Mughal tradition. Some records state that its design was the original one for the Sultan Abdul Samad Building. Later, the building served as the KL Memorial Library until the domed Kuala Lumpur City Library was erected next to it. Today, the building hosts the **Kuala Lumpur City Gallery ❹** (daily 9am–6.30pm) providing some tourist information and some city history, but is mostly a showcase and gift centre of the wood veneer souvenir company Arch. Also worth seeing is a wonderful

⊙ ONION DOMES

The onion domes used in KL's colonial architecture are the most obvious structural representation of Islam today. Found on virtually every mosque in the country, the dome was brought to the Malay Archipelago by Western colonialists. Domes are believed to have first appeared in the Middle East; a roof feature that was born of necessity. The lack of timber to make flat roofs meant that mud bricks had to be used. This adaptation spread under the Byzantine Empire, and in the 7th century Arabs used this feature for the Dome of the Rock in Jerusalem, one of the holiest sites in Islam. The shape of the domes in KL's colonial core is derived from the Islamic Mughal tradition that, in turn, adopted this feature from Persian and Uzbek architecture.

miniature model of Dataran Merdeka and a massive model of greater KL with an audio-visual presentation (entry fee applies).

RAILWAY BUILDINGS
There is another set of lovely Mughal-style buildings about 1km (0.6 miles) south of the colonial core on Jalan Sultan Hishamuddin. The **Railway Administration Building** (Bangunan KTM Berhad) and the **Old KL Railway**

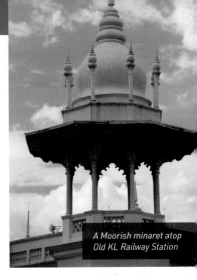

A Moorish minaret atop Old KL Railway Station

Station ❺ (Stesen Keretapi Kuala Lumpur) are stunning architectural pieces; showcases of pillared pavilions, decorative arches and spires. While the former is still used as the offices of KTM (Malaysian Railways), the latter has been left underused since 2001, when interstate rail services were transferred to the ultra-modern KL Sentral transport hub. Now, the only departures from here are KTM Komuter trains and the luxurious Eastern & Oriental Express (www.belmond.com/eastern-and-oriental-express) on its Singapore-Bangkok route.

CENTRAL MARKET
For souvenir-hunters and art buffs there is **Central Market ❻** (Pasar Seni; www.centralmarket.com.my; daily 10am–9.30pm). Located south of Old Market Square on Jalan Hang Kasturi, this was once the city's largest wet-produce market. Its Art Deco features were conserved when it was converted into a

Jalan Petaling's gateway

shopping mall in the 1980s. Many goods from Malaysia and elsewhere in Asia can be bought here, from handicrafts to clothes. Its multi-level arts space, **The Annexe**, has a varied programme of innovative performances, exhibitions and film screenings. Along the side of Central Market is Kasturi Walk, a pedestrian mall adorned with an outsized *wau* (kite), with more souvenir stalls. Cultural performances are held nightly at 9pm.

PETALING STREET

Of the streets in the original Chinese quarter of Kuala Lumpur, Petaling Street is the best known among tourists. However, the whole area is worth exploring as it is full of temples, clan-houses and a bustling local community that date back to KL's origins. This enclave is still evolving, with the emergence of a new migrant social centre.

SIN SZE SI YA TEMPLE

One of the city's most important Taoist temples honours its most famous son, Yap Ah Loy, the Chinese community leader who prevented early KL from disappearing back into the jungle. The **Sin Sze Si Ya Temple** ❼ (113A Jalan Tun H.S. Lee; daily 7am–5pm) is hidden from view except for an ornate, painted doorway with a relief carving of a dragon. The temple was built in 1864 by Yap himself, then the *Kapitan Cina* (Chinese Captain) of KL. He wanted to honour two of his comrades, Sin Sze Ya and Si Sze Ya, who became venerated as deities after their deaths. Their altars occupy the main hall.

After his own death in 1885, Yap was also deified. The altar dedicated to him is on the left-hand side of the main hall. A bust of Yap sits nearby. If the temple seems oddly placed within its courtyard, with its entrance facing a corner, this is because it was built according to strict *feng shui* principles.

MIGRANT ENCLAVE

East of this temple along Lebuh Pudu and Jalan Tun Tan Siew Sin (popularly known as Jalan Silang) is a lively social centre for Nepalis, Burmese and Bangladeshis; three large migrant worker groups. KL's economy relies heavily on over 100,000 migrant workers, with the majority coming from Indonesia. This enclave provides a fascinating window into the dynamic enriching of Malaysian life and culture. Here, you will see signs that are entirely in Nepali and Burmese script. Depending on their target clientele, you will find stores stocked with Bangladeshi music and videos, *The Myanmar Times* and the sarong-like *lung ji*, or the popular Nepali fried *momo* pastry, and soap and shampoo from Kathmandu. On Sundays and public holidays the area is totally jammed.

PETALING STREET BAZAAR

South of Jalan Tun Tan Cheng Lock, in an area dominated by pre-war Chinese-style shophouses, is the start of the city's most famous street bazaar. Referred to by the name of the main thoroughfare that it occupies, **Petaling Street** ❽ sits in a bustling part of KL, bookended by gateways bearing the street's name. The bazaar also occupies the perpendicular Jalan Hang Lekir, where there are eateries and shops selling Chinese snacks and sweets.

Also known as Chinatown, Petaling Street is reputedly where the best Chinese street food can be found, from all sorts of noodles to pork ribs soup *(bak kut teh)* and roasted meat snacks. There are *dim sum* from 6am, mooncakes for the autumnal Mooncake Festival, and bittersweet herbal brews to cure all sorts of ailments at the roadside medicinal drinks stalls.

⊘ THE ART OF TEA

The tea shops in this area are a great place to learn about Chinese tea. Attendants explain the different types of tea and demonstrate Chinese tea culture, which is less well known and elaborate than the Japanese counterpart but equally fascinating. Shops sell a range of Chinese teas, as well as porcelain and clay teapots and associated paraphernalia.

A popular tea-shop chain is Purple Cane, which has branches throughout the city, including at 6 Jalan Panggung, near Jalan Balai Polis (daily 11am–7pm). Purple Cane also has a restaurant (daily 11am–10pm) in the Chinese Assembly Hall on Jalan Maharajalela across from the Guan Yin Temple, where every dish cooked uses Chinese tea as an ingredient.

From 10am, displays of largely counterfeit branded goods are laid out. There are also souvenirs, fruits and munchies on sale. Come night-time, the atmosphere turns electric in the fluorescent glow as more bodies amass and the sense of cut-throat commerce intensifies. Still, bargain-hunters are likely to be in their element, although one must bargain hard. Non-shoppers may find the market's calmer

A worshipper at Si Sze Ye Temple

daytime variant more manageable. Respite can be found at a red table-clothed table along the dining stretch of Jalan Hang Lekir leading to Jalan Sultan.

AROUND PETALING STREET

West of Jalan Petaling, the stretch of **Jalan Tun H.S. Lee** ❾ from Jalan Sultan to Jalan Tun Tan Siew Sin is packed with interesting sights. This historic street was once known as High Street because it was literally higher than the surroundings and therefore less prone to floods. Its walkways are still of different heights as previous owners kept raising them to avoid their premises being flooded. Its lovely shophouses go back to the 1800s and several have been turned into backpacker outfits.

At the Jalan Hang Lekir corner is the **Lee Rubber Building**, which houses Popular Bookshop. Built by one of the country's

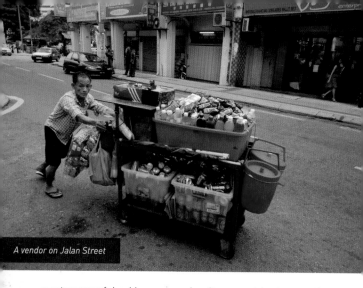

A vendor on Jalan Street

most successful rubber companies, its geometric shape and designs are classic Art Deco, a decorative architectural style that was employed throughout Malaya in the 1930s.

Diagonally opposite this building is one of the oldest Cantonese temples in the city, the **Guan Di Temple** (daily 7am– 7pm). This 1888 place of worship honours the red-faced God of War and Literature, Guan Di, whose statue is located in the main hall. It was built by the Kwong Siew Association, a clan association representing many of Kuala Lumpur's original Cantonese-speaking Chinese families.

Opposite this temple, back on the same side as the Lee Rubber Building, is a key Hindu temple, the **Sri Maha Mariamman Temple** (Sun–Thu 6am-8.30pm, Fri 6am– 9.30pm, Sat 6am–9pm). Built in 1873, it houses a statue of the deity Murugan which is drawn on a silver chariot during the Thaipusam festival to its sister temple in Batu Caves (see page

76). The temple's impressive gateway tower is adorned with intricately carved statues of Hindu deities.

South of Jalan Tun H.S. Lee is **Gurdwara Sahib Polis** (6 Jalan Balai Polis; daily 9am–6pm), a Sikh temple located within a police compound and painted in the blue of Malaysian police buildings. Sikhs were first brought from India to the Malay States by the British to be part of the police force, and once made up its majority. Opposite it is the **Old China Café** (www.oldchina.com.my; daily 11am–10.30pm), which occupies the old guildhall of the Selangor and Federal Territory Laundry Association. It now serves Nonya food but beautifully preserves its 1930s atmosphere, complete with wooden doors, giant *feng shui* mirrors and framed photos. Upstairs is a gallery of antiques.

CHAN SHE SHU YUEN

At the southern end of Jalan Petaling is the **Chan She Shu Yuen Clan Association Building** ❿ (daily 8am–6pm). This clan association was established in 1896 to serve early Chinese migrants to Malaya bearing the surname Chan and its variations of Chen and Tan. Although the paint has faded, this remains one of the most decorated clan association buildings in town. Its roof features decorative curved gables, and its external walls are covered

Detail on the Sri Maha Mariamman Temple

The Chan She Shu Yuen Clan Association Building

with remarkably detailed porcelain friezes depicting Chinese mythology, popular dramas and history.

Across the road from this building and near the pedestrian bridge across Jalan Maharajalela is a flight of steps guarded by a pair of stone lions. At the top of the stairs is **Guan Yin Temple** (daily 7am–5pm). This small Hokkien temple (built in 1880) is named after Guan Yin, the Goddess of Mercy, one of the most popular deities worshipped by local Buddhists. The statue of Guan Yin here depicts her in a thousand-armed and thousand-eyed manifestation, representing her omniscience. This is one of the few Hokkien temples in town and sports a curved roof typical of such temples.

From the side entrance of the Guan Yin Temple, steps lead to the Maharajalela Monorail Station and a car park on the left. Beyond this stands the **Stadium Merdeka**. Purpose-built to celebrate the proclamation of independence of Malaya on 31 August 1957, this humble building was the location of the most iconic moment in the country's modern history: when the first prime minister, Tunku Abdul Rahman, punched the air and shouted *'Merdeka'* ('independence'). The venue of great sporting events thereafter; the revered boxer Muhammad Ali fought here in 1975. The stadium has been painstakingly restored to its original shape – a triumph for conservation in development-crazy

KL – although the 118-storey KL118 tower (due to be completed in 2024), threatens to render it inconspicuous.

JALAN MASJID INDIA AND KAMPUNG BARU

North of the Klang and Gombak river confluence are chaotic and colourful enclaves with strong Malay and Indian characters. These are centred around Jalan Masjid India and north of this, the sprawling 90-hectare (220-acre) preserve of Kampung Baru, Kuala Lumpur's oldest Malay settlement.

JALAN MASJID INDIA

Indian businesses have had a long history in KL, as is evident in the area around **Jalan Masjid India** ⓫. On Jalan Melayu (Malay Street), one of the city's original streets, sits one of its oldest businesses at No. 5 and 7, **the Goodluck Trading Company**. This wholesale business was set up in 1895 by Indians from Chennai. The business is now run by the fourth-generation descendants of the original merchants. Their speciality is *kain pelikat chop gadja*, high-quality checked hand-loomed sarongs for men. These cloths are imported from Pulicat, an area near Chennai whose valuable textiles once funded 17th-century Dutch trade in the Malay Archipelago.

There is a good value bazaar (daily 9am–10pm) which runs in an 'L' shape along the Jalan Melayu

Clanhouses

Chinese clanhouses belong to clan associations; community groups formed in the 19th century by new Chinese migrants to the country. The associations provided financial, education, employment and welfare services to newcomers, so clanhouses comprised not just temples, but accommodation and meeting halls too.

Men in sarongs

The cotton kain pelikat sarong is a favourite lounging and sleeping attire among Malaysian men, although younger urbanites have eschewed it. Malay men also wear kain pelikat when praying at the mosque. This is the best time to see the diversity of designs and patterns in which this humble cloth comes.

sidewalk from the Masjid Jamek LRT station and the pedestrianised first stretch of Jalan Masjid India. Shopping is better on the five-foot way of Wisma Yakin (daily 9am–9.30pm), to the bazaar's east. It is an emporium of Malay shops where you can buy good local and Indonesian batiks, traditional herbal concoctions for health and beauty, and other Malay goods.

To the west of the bazaar is the brown slate-walled **Masjid India**, an Indian Muslim mosque, whose original building was erected in the 19th century, after which the street is named. Here, religious services are conducted in Arabic and Tamil; it has a unique Indian-Muslim atmosphere. Although it is open only to Muslim worshippers, at 1.30pm on Fridays, the entire bazaar area outside the mosque is filled with worshippers attending Friday prayers. There are good photo opportunities here, but discretion is strongly advised.

SEMUA HOUSE AND PLAZA CITY ONE

The rest of Jalan Masjid India comprises shops selling Malay outfits, scarves, *songkok* (Muslim male headgear) and sarongs, as well as Indian outfits and household products. Particularly dazzling are the lavish window displays of gold jewellery in ethnic and contemporary designs that are imported from Dubai and India.

At the end of Jalan Masjid India are a couple of shopping malls. Directly facing the junction is **Semua House** (daily

10am–10pm), a one-stop shop for Malay weddings, with everything from fabrics and gift baskets to fake flowers and bridal outfits for rent. **Madras Store** (daily 10.30am–8.30pm), opposite it, and **Plaza City One** (Mon–Fri 10am–10pm, Sat–Sun 9am–11pm), to its right, are both high-rise Little Indias, offering traditional and Bollywood-style clothing, accessories and *mehndi* (henna-painting) services.

Opposite Plaza City One and through a lane sits a tiny Hindu temple, **Sri Pathra Kaliamman Temple**. Its main deity is the green-faced Kali the Destroyer, but cobra-shaped worship paraphernalia appease an ancient cobra said to visit the temple. Noteworthy is the century-old Kali statue at the back entrance. The temple is often busy as it serves as the area's place of worship for business owners and staff.

Men on their way to prayers at Masjid India

JALAN TUANKU ABDUL RAHMAN

Parallel to Jalan Masjid India is **Jalan Tuanku Abdul Rahman**, one of the longest streets in the city, and broad to boot. Originally called Batu Road, it was built to link pre-independence Kuala Lumpur to the tin mines in Batu. Stores sprang up along this road and it soon became the main shopping street. After independence, it was renamed after the first *Agong* (King) of Malaysia, and is fondly known as Jalan TAR.

In 1920, the **Coliseum Cinema** at No. 96 was built. Not only has the cinema survived threats to demolish it for redevelopment purposes, it continues to serve its original function. Housed in a lovely neoclassical building, the cinema shows mainly Malay and Tamil films.

At 98–100 Jalan Tuanku Abdul Rahman is the **Coliseum Café and Hotel** ⑫, one of KL's favourite institutions. Built in 1921, the establishment's decor and mismatched furniture and fittings are quaintly nostalgic. Its bar, now frequented by lawyers and tourists, was once a popular drinking hole for prosperous colonial planters, tin miners and traders. The upper floors once provided basic accommodation for those who did not quite make the cut for the finer hotels in the colonial quarter. It is now an atmospheric

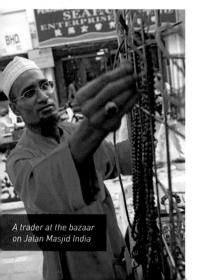
A trader at the bazaar on Jalan Masjid India

budget hotel. The restaurant (www.coliseum1921.com; daily 10am–10pm) continues to dish up a pre-independence menu of tasty sizzling steaks and baked crab.

FABRIC HOUSES

It is immediately evident that the stretch of Jalan Tuanku Abdul Rahman north of the Coliseum to the Sogo Department Store is a centre for fabrics and textiles. Almost every other shop features fabrics draped over dummies, cloth hanging from ceiling to floor, or endless shelves filled with bales of cotton, chiffon and other fluttery material. A whole gamut of stores, from retail to wholesale, has an address here.

Kamdar (daily 10am–10pm), a popular chain selling afford-able textiles, furnishings and ready-to-wear traditional Malay and Indian clothing, has three outlets along this road alone (Nos 113, 171, 429–35). Posher outlets include **Gulati's Silk House** at No. 162–164; its high-end chain store, **Euro Moda** at No. 126–128; and **Mayasilk** at No. 140. These outlets are where you are most likely to spot high-society *Mak Datin* (wealthy, older Malay women), starlets and politicians' wives receiving meticulous service and tailoring advice.

KAMPUNG BARU

North of this area is Kampung Baru, where doorways are adorned with the *asalamualaikum* welcome sign in Arabic, and children in traditional Malay dress make their way to or from religious classes. Surrounded by skyscrapers, it stubbornly retains a unique character that is Muslim and communal. Many of the original owners have in fact moved out and rented or sold their homes to Indonesians.

The gentle bustle of **Jalan Raja Muda Musa** ⑬ is typical of much of Kampung Baru. Here, the street is lined with eateries

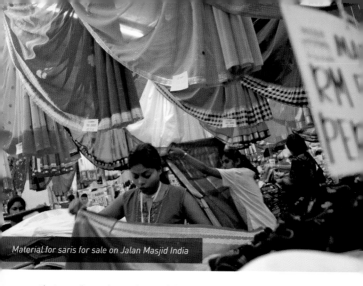

Material for saris for sale on Jalan Masjid India

that are always busy, day or night. All kinds of people come here from far and wide for the best home-cooked Malay food in town.

Here they will find infinite variations of the rice-and-spice *nasi lemak*; specialities from their hometowns like the northern *laksa*, spicy and sour rice noodles, and the east coast *nasi kerabu* herb rice delicacy; as well as regional favourites like the rice-and-curry *nasi padang* from Sumatra and Javanese grilled meats. Equally abundant are snacks of local cakes or *kuih*, the most common featuring glutinous rice, coconut milk or bananas.

The eateries are simple, with food laid out on tables, and plastic chairs and tables prettied up with a vase of artificial flowers. Most are also set up in the compounds of houses, giving diners a *kampung* (village) feel. While many of Kampung Baru's houses are now partially or entirely made of brick, there are still some original stilted wooden gems to be seen. However, the ultra-modern Petronas Twin Towers in the background are a constant reminder of the transitory nature of old neighbourhoods, especially ones occupying prime land like Kampung Baru.

JALAN RAJA ALANG

Jalan Raja Alang, which connects to Jalan Raja Muda Musa, is a slightly quieter street. **No. 60** is a large house that is a beautiful example of traditional Malay architecture, despite being painted a garish green. It has a raised central *serambi* reception area flanked by two curving stairways and fronted by ceiling-to-floor windows for ventilation.

⊘ RELIGIOUS SCHOOLS

Kampung Baru is where you are most likely to see children attending Islamic religious schools or *madrasah*. The give-aways are their uniforms. For boys this comprises of *songkok* (Malay headgear) and elasticated *sampin* (a wrap worn over trousers), and for girls, *tudung* (headscarf) and *baju kurung* (long-sleeved tunic and a sarong).

Islamic religious schools were the first educational institutions for Malays in pre-British Malaya. They were housed in vernacular-style buildings, hence their moniker of *Sekolah Pondok* (Hut School). Today, religious schools are usually confined to rural areas. Students learn subjects like Arabic and Islamic history and law. However, graduates of these schools are not recognised for entry into local universities, and must pursue tertiary education in the Middle East. The secular education system includes compulsory Islamic religious classes for Muslim students, but some parents send their children for supplementary religious instruction in mosques.

At the corner of Jalan Raja Alang and Jalan Raja Abdullah is the **Masjid Jamek Kampung Baru** (Kampung Baru Jamek Mosque; daily 9am–5pm, except prayer times). Built around 1924, it was one of the first concrete structures erected in the quarter. It has since been renovated, and the latest addition is a gateway adorned with a turquoise ceramic pattern of Middle Eastern origin. The mosque briefly became a rallying point during the ethnic clashes of 13 May 1969 (see page 22), when politically motivated troublemakers brought about its symbolic association with strife by using it as a gathering point for protests.

Fortunately, peace now reigns at the mosque, and it has become more famous for feeding the masses. During the Muslim fasting month of Ramadan, the mosque dishes out endless bowls of *bubur lambuk*, a peppery rice porridge cooked with minced beef. The massive cook-out was initiated by two imams in the 1950s and is part of community service by the area's residents. Ramadan is a particularly lively time to visit this street, as a riot of mainly food stalls beneath colourful umbrellas do a roaring trade during the month-long **Pasar Ramadan**, literally 'Ramadan Market' (3pm–midnight). The atmosphere is festive as

⊙ NATIONAL ART GALLERY

Located northwest of Kampung Baru is the National Art Gallery (Balai Seni Negara; www.artgallery.gov.my; daily 10am–6pm). This beautiful contemporary space elegantly incorporates elements of traditional Malay architecture in a multi-storey space. It has six galleries and the ground-floor main gallery showcases works from the institution's 2,500-piece permanent collection.

Muslims throng the market to buy speciality Ramadan delicacies or break their fast (*buka puasa*) during the evening *maghrib* prayer time around 7.30pm. The date of Ramadan changes each year, as it follows the lunar calendar.

In this largely Muslim neighbourhood stands a Sikh gurdwara, the impressive **Guru Nanak Darbaar Gurdwara Sahib** (open only to worshippers). Standing out on Jalan Alang, west of

Outside Masjid Jamek Kampung Baru

the Kampung Baru Jamek Mosque, are its squat Indo-Persian domes, adorned at the base with lotus petals; this design predates the Mughal domes adopted by the British for the colonial core. The central dome has a miniature umbrella called a *chatri*, symbolising shelter for mankind. Its main prayer hall is the largest in Southeast Asia.

LAKE GARDENS

West of the colonial core spreads a 104-hectare (257-acre) urban park fondly called the **Lake Gardens** ⑭ although its formal name is the Taman Botani Perdana (Perdana Botanical Gardens; www.klbotanicalgarden.gov.my; daily 7am–8pm; guided walks are free Mon–Fri 8–10am). The brainchild of a former British State Treasurer 140 years ago, the Lake Gardens has become an important recreation area and green lung for the residents of Kuala Lumpur. Here pathways meander through lawns, cultivated gardens and animal sanctuaries, as well as museums. Popular with exercise enthusiasts, from joggers to tai chi exponents, weekends, especially, draw mums, dads and kids, with maids in tow and picnic baskets in hand; this is a great place to watch Malaysian families at play.

FLORA AND FAUNA

From the main entrance, Jalan Cenderasari leads to the **Butterfly Park** (www.klbutterflypark.com; daily 9am–6pm). Here, in pretty surroundings, an extremely humid environment keeps thousands of plants and butterflies of all shapes and colours happy.

In the Lake Gardens

The western artery of Jalan Cenderamulia leads to the gorgeous **Conservatory and Herbal Garden** (daily 7am–6pm) in the northwestern corner of the park. While the Conservatory – one of the original features in the gardens – showcases beautifully laid-out plant collections, the herbal section provides insights into local herbs and spices.

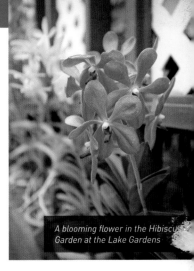

A blooming flower in the Hibiscus Garden at the Lake Gardens

Heading southwards, Jalan Kebun Bunga leads to the **lake.** Close to the lake are the pretty **Oasis Garden**, with its shady foliage and waterfall, and the **heliconia** and **ginger** (Zingiberales) collections. Cutting east across the square will lead to the **Deer Park** (daily 10am–6pm). This is a rare opportunity to view the mouse deer, the world's smallest deer, which is the size of a cat and extremely shy. The park's breeding success has been high, so lucky visitors might just spot a baby. Visitors may also feed Mauritian and Dutch deer here.

Meanwhile, off the eastern artery of Jalan Cenderawasih are the **Orchid & Hibiscus Gardens** (daily 9am–6pm). The latter garden is a tribute to Malaysia's national flower, the hibiscus (*bunga raya*), and features 2,500 hibiscus plants from all over the world. A pathway at the back of this garden leads to the Orchid Garden. Malaysia has one of the most diverse orchid species collections in the world, and this garden shows off a mixture of wild and cultivated species, of which some specimens are for sale.

Opposite the Orchid Garden is the **Kuala Lumpur Bird Park** (www.klbirdpark.com; daily 9am–6pm). This 8-hectare (20-acre) covered aviary is home to over 200 bird species, most housed in display areas. Do not miss the hornbill section, where you can get close-up views of these large black-and-white creatures with prominent beaks and magnificent tails.

INDOOR ATTRACTIONS

West of the lake on Persiaran Mahameru is an elegant colonial mansion called **Carcosa Seri Negara**, now a luxury boutique hotel. The mock-Tudor Carcosa, which was built in 1896, was once the residence of top British officials. Partake in luxurious English afternoon tea on its verandas (daily 3–6pm) while looking out on manicured lawns.

National Mosque

Otherwise, from the Deer Park, continue along Jalan Perdana past the Tun Razak Memorial, which commemorates the second prime minister. After about 500 m/yds, you will come to the **Planetarium Negara** (National Planetarium; www.planetariumnegara.gov.my; Tue–Sun 9am–4.30pm). The planetarium has a 36-cm (14-inch) telescope, houses the Arianne IV space engine that launched Malaysia's first satellite and has screenings of large-format documentaries. Its well-designed garden is scattered with replicas of ancient observatories.

A pedestrian bridge behind the Planetarium leads to the **National Museum** ⑮ (Muzium Negara; www.muziumnegara.gov.my; daily 9am–6pm; free guided tours daily at 10am), a fine example of post-independence architecture. Accessible via a walkway from the Planetarium, the building was completed in 1963 and is modelled after Kedah's Balai Besar, a 19th-century Thai-influenced audience hall for sultans. Two gigantic batik murals depict the country's history, culture, politics and economy.

Head back to the Planetarium and walk towards Jalan Lembah Perdana. At the southeastern end of the Lake Gardens stands the excellent **Islamic Arts Museum Malaysia** ⑯ (Muzium Kesenian Islam Malaysia; www.iamm.org.my; daily 10am–6pm). This private museum has a fine collection of artefacts and art objects from all over the Islamic world. Of note are Asian and Southeast Asian Islamic art. The building itself is a beauty, a dignified contemporary space that incorporates Iranian and Central Asian architecture.

Opposite this museum is the **Masjid Negara** (National Mosque; Sat–Thu 9am–1pm, 2.30–4pm and 5.30–7pm, Fri closed in the morning). Completed in 1965 and capable of holding 15,000 people, it was one of the first buildings constructed to reflect statehood. It sports a unique circular blue-ridged roof symbolising an open umbrella, geometric latticework and white marble.

Tram Ride

For a quick overview of the gardens, take the tram (daily 9.30am–12.30pm and 2.30–5.30pm), which covers all sights, including the National Mosque.

BRICKFIELDS

South of the Lake Gardens is the atmospheric old neighbourhood of Brickfields, home to a mainly Indian community and an impressive number of places of worship. The area was thus named because it was here in the late 19th century that clay was dug up and bricks manufactured to rebuild Kuala Lumpur after fires and floods destroyed the settlement's wooden buildings. After that, Brickfields became a centre for the railways and government quarters for local civil servants. Since most colonial railway workers and civil servants were Tamils from South India and Sri Lanka, the area has an Indian flavour. The northern clay pit has been redeveloped into the ultra-modern KL Sentral, a self-contained city of offices, condominiums and hotels.

JALAN SCOTT AND JALAN THAMBIPILLAI

Jalan Scott ⓱ is where the Brickfields township first took shape and has become a centre for Hindu temples. At one end of this

---

◉ NATIONAL MONUMENT

North of the Lake Gardens across Jalan Parliament is the National Monument (Tugu Peringatan Negara; daily 7am–6pm), which commemorates servicemen who died during the communist insurgency of 1948–60. It was modelled after the Iwo Jima Memorial in the US. Steps lead down to a cenotaph commemorating the soldiers of the two World Wars.

Down the hill is the ASEAN Sculpture Garden (daily 24 hours), whose sculptures symbolise the mainly economic alliance among the 10 nations of the Association of Southeast Asian Nations.

road is the important **Sri Kandaswamy Kovil** (www.srikandaswamykovil.org; Mon–Thu 5.30am–1pm, 5–9pm; Fri–Sun 5.30am–1.30pm, 5–9.30pm), founded by the local Jaffna Sri Lankan community in 1902. This is a Murugan temple, which sports an impressive gateway and marble and gold fittings. Down the road from it are three temples.

A detail on Sri Kandaswamy Kovil Temple at Brickfields

The newest one, the simple **Sri Krishna Temple** (www.sreekrishnatemple.com; daily 6am–noon, 6–9pm), honours the blue god, and features a statue of him as well as two incarnations of his consort, Lakshmi. Next door is the newly enlarged **Arulmegu Sree Veera Hanuman Temple** (www.veerahanuman.com; daily 7am–10pm), which honours Hanuman, the Monkey God. Best known from the epic *Ramayana*, Hanuman is revered for courage and devotion. This temple houses five statues of the deity. The last of the trio is another small temple that is in a rather sorry state. The **Sri Maha Muneswarar Temple** (daily 6–10am, 4–10pm) features the trident-carrying and *dhoti*-clad Muneeswarar, also known as Muniandi, a guardian Tamil deity originally worshipped in plantations and villages.

Among the pre-war shophouses facing these temples, **Wei-Ling Gallery** at No. 8 shows a beautiful reuse of space after the building was gutted by fire (www.weiling-gallery.com; Mon–Fri

10am–6pm, Sat 10am–5pm). This art gallery sells contemporary local and international art.

Southwest of Jalan Scott is **Jalan Thambipillai**, which runs through a busier part of Brickfields. A notable feature here is the large number of blind people; they frequent the Malaysian Association of the Blind, which is next to the Tun Sambanthan Monorail station. Some are trained masseurs who work in the massage parlours along Jalan Thambipillai and the streets off it.

There are plenty of Chinese and Indian food choices here, from snacks to hawker fare and restaurants. On the corner of Jalan Thambipillai and Jalan Tun Sambanthan 4, opposite the YMCA, is a popular sidewalk *goreng pisang* (banana fritters) stall (daily 12.30–6pm). It does a roaring trade selling not just the banana snack but also the *kuih bakul* yam fritters and curry puffs.

Down the road is a 50-year-old Buddhist temple called the **Sam Kow Tong** (Three Teachings Temple), whose back faces the road. Surprisingly, located next to it is a red-light area in the shape of a dozen seedy shop lots.

JALAN BERHALA

Jalan Thambipillai leads to **Jalan Berhala ⑱**, a U-shaped road formerly known as Temple Road, which is packed with pre-World War II places of worship, as well as a host of schools, bungalows and flats. A key temple here is the **Sri Sakti Karpaga Vinayagar Temple** (daily 6am–noon, 6–9pm). It is the country's only temple hosting the Elephant God Ganesha holding a Sivalingam, a symbol synonymous with the principal god Siva. During the festival celebrating Ganesha, which falls in the Tamil month of Aavani (Aug–Sept), this statue is drawn by elephants in a chariot around Brickfields.

Further down Jalan Berhala at No. 114–116 is the **Temple of Fine Arts** (www.tfa.org.my), a premium classical-Indian

The Hundred Quarters

performance arts centre for dance, instrumental and voice classes. Visitors may request a tour of the venue, which is brimming with activity on weekends. The arts centre stages large-scale and elaborate performances, as well as smaller ones, year-round. It also has a lovely gift shop and hosts the Annalakshmi Riverside café and fancier Annalakshmi Restaurant (www.annalakshmi.com.my; Tue–Sun 11.30am–3pm, 6.30–10pm), both of which serve home-cooked vegetarian food.

Round the bend is the **Maha Vihara Temple** (www.buddhist mahavihara.org; daily 6am–10pm), one of KL's most important Buddhist temples, founded by Singhalese who were brought here by the British to be civil servants. Modest in appearance, the temple assumes an electric atmosphere come Wesak Day (May), which marks the birth, enlightenment and death of the Buddha. This temple is the start and end-point of a night-time float procession featuring hundreds of devotees.

At the corner of Jalan Berhala and Jalan Sultan Abdul Samad is the **Lutheran Cathedral** (www.elcm.org.my), one of many churches in Brickfields, representing a large array of denominations. These include the Catholic Church of the Holy Rosary, the Tamil Methodist Church and Our Lady of Fatima Church. Services are held in English as well as Tamil and/or Mandarin.

JALAN TUN SAMBANTHAN

Zigzag past the Lutheran Cathedral back to the main road, Jalan Tun Sambanthan. Enroute are the **Hundred Quarters** on Jalan Chan Ah Tong and Jalan Rozario. Set in straight rows, these 1915 British-built quarters housed middle-class civil servants, and are built of concrete, which was considered a luxury at the time. Barely changed over the years, they continue to house a lively community of civil servants.

Fronting Jalan Tun Sambanthan is the **Vivekananda Ashram**, established for followers of the influential spiritual leader of the Vedanta branch of Hindu philosophy. A statue of Vivekananda stands in front of this long pink-and-white building.

Bangsar

Northwest of Brickfields is the suburb of Bangsar, which has some of the most expensive real estate in Kuala Lumpur. Its two main entertainment areas, Bangsar Baru and the Bangsar Shopping Centre, are dense with chic bars, shops and eateries filled with the fashion set.

West of this building on Jalan Tun Sambanthan and Jalan Travers are rows of **shophouses** offering everything from Carnatic music to Indian mangoes and lovely South Indian banana-leaf meals. A misguided political attempt in 2010 to recognise the Malaysian Indian population has seen

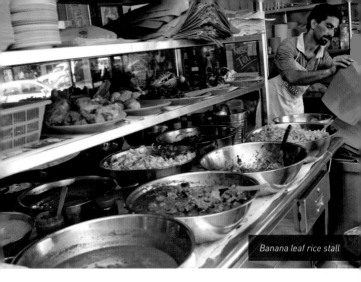

Banana leaf rice stall

the addition to this stretch of Jalan Tun Sambanthan of garish colours and gateways announcing it as 'Little India'. Still, look past the gaudiness to explore spice shops such as Asokan (No. 225; daily 10am–10pm) and Modern Store (No. 233; daily 10am–10pm), buy a sweet or savoury snack at Venusitas (No. 270; daily 9am–10.45pm) and walk through the narrow lane of garland sellers (between No. 245 and 251; daily 8.30am–11pm).

At the end of the Little India stretch on Jalan Tun Sambanthan Satu is **St Mary's Orthodox Syrian Cathedral** (www.orthodoxchurchmy.com; Sun 8am–noon). This faith has origins in Kerala, and traces its roots to the evangelism of Thomas the Apostle in the 1st century AD. The church was the first in the order to be consecrated outside India, in 1958, and the liturgy is Syrian Orthodox. Priests and deacons wear the elaborate vestments unique to this church.

KL SENTRAL

Looming over Brickfields is KL Sentral, the high-density self-contained city of offices, condominiums and hotels, which also hosts the city's railway hub. The architecture and vibe here could not be of greater contrast to Brickfields. Here, there are futuristic skyscrapers such as 348 Sentral, whose concertinaed, glass-clad towers feature two international chain hotels boasting ultra-modern interiors, chic bars and restaurants, as well as resort-like swimming pools lined with palm trees up in the sky.

To the consternation of conservationists, the high-rise, modernisation bug has started infecting Brickfields on the other side of the road. Tradition seems to be grimly hanging on, but the pressure of modernisation is palpable.

KLCC

Soaring 452m (1,483ft) into the sky, the iconic Petronas Twin Towers are the literal high point of the city and of Kuala Lumpur's new heart, the Kuala Lumpur City Centre (KLCC). Like KL Sentral, this 40-hectare (100-acre) area is a redevelopment exercise, occupying what used to be the Selangor Turf Club. This self-contained city will eventually comprise tower blocks serving as corporate offices, hotels and luxury accommodation, all surrounding an artily landscaped park. KLCC anchors the city's business and financial district, called the Golden Triangle, and is the place to find the best shopping and nightlife.

PETRONAS TWIN TOWERS

Clad entirely in steel and glass, the **Petronas Twin Towers** ⑲ are quite an amazing sight, especially set against the velvet night sky. It is particularly mesmerising when there is a full moon and, if you get your vantage point right, the yellow orb appears

The Golden Triangle's skyline at night

suspended between the lighted spires. The Twin Towers were built at the end of the Mahathir administration as a monument that would befit an economic Asian Tiger nation making its presence felt in the world. The towers held the Guinness Book of Records' world's-tallest-building record between 1996 and 2003. They remain among the tallest structures in the world.

A breathtaking piece of engineering that consumed unimaginable amounts of concrete, steel and glass, the Twin Towers' architecture, by the renowned New York-based Cesar Pelli, also encapsulates Malaysian sensibilities. The basic shape of each tower is an eight-point star formed from two interlocking squares, a popular Islamic architectural design. Semicircles are superimposed on the inner angles of the squares. Steel sections working as sun-shading devices add to the unique lines and shadows on the buildings' facades. There are 88 storeys in all, signifying 'double luck', a Chinese belief.

The Twin Towers house offices, including the headquarters of state oil and gas giant Petronas, but are not open to the public. However, there is an immensely popular 45-minute semi-guided tour that goes up to the double-deck **skybridge** on Levels 41 and 42, as well as up to **Level 86**, the topmost level open to visitors (www.petronastwintowers.com.my; Tue–Sun 9am–9pm, Fri closed between 1–2.30pm) for panoramic views of the city. Only 400 tickets are sold a day to walk-ins and another 400 are reserved for advance purchases. Tickets are available on the day from 8.30am at the information desk in Tower 2.

Tower 2 also hosts the custom-built **Petronas Philharmonic Hall** (Dewan Filharmonik Petronas; www.mpo.com.my; Tue–Sat 10.30am–6.30pm, 9pm on performance days, noon to

⊙ TOP VIEWS

Visitors often like to photograph the Petronas Twin Towers from the Suria Esplanade, but the best views of the towers are from the KLCC Park, Jalan Ampang, Jalan Tun Razak and the hotels around it. Stunning night-time views are on offer from chic rooftop bars like the Luna Bar at the Pacific Regency Hotel Suites, the Sky Lounge at Hotel Maya (hotel guests only) and the Sky Lounge at the Trader's Hotel.

The best views of the KL skyline are actually from the Kuala Lumpur Elevated Highway, parallel to Jalan Ampang, where you can see both of the city's iconic towers; note, though, that pedestrians are not allowed on the highway and drivers are not allowed to stop.

The best times to photograph the Twin Towers are during the spectacular fireworks displays on New Year's Eve and National Day (31 Aug).

performance time on Sun; dress codes apply). The interesting programme features not only the Malaysian Philharmonic Orchestra but also international musicians ranging in musical styles from chamber and contemporary classical to jazz and world music.

In Petrosains

SURIA KLCC

The base of the towers is occupied by a classy six-storey shopping centre, **Suria KLCC** (daily 10am–10pm), which has over 270 speciality shops and restaurants, as well as cinemas and other attractions. At No. 341-43 is **Galeri Petronas** (www.galeripetronas.com. my; 10am–8pm), an elegant gallery exhibiting modern visual arts particularly from Malaysian artists. The permanent collection of Malaysian art from the 20th century is one of the largest in the country.

Petronas also runs an excellent interactive museum on science and the oil and gas industry for families on levels 4 and 5. **Petrosains** (www.petrosains.com.my; Tue–Fri 9.30am–5.30pm; Sat–Sun 9.30am–6.30pm) is on the sixth floor. On the ground floor is another beautifully laid out, if commercial, gallery of Southeast Asian handicrafts and products, **Aseana** (G16-18).

At the front of the shopping centre is an esplanade, which faces a choreographed fountain display. When lit up at night it is especially pretty. The esplanade is also lined with trendy cafés and bars, great for people-watching over a latte or wine. A view of the fountains and esplanade can also be had from the upstairs restaurants on this side of Suria.

KLCC PARK

The fountains sit in a lake within the lovely **KLCC Park** (daily 7am–10pm), a 20-hectare (50-acre) garden designed by the late Brazilian landscape artist Roberto Burle Marx. Among the vegetation are about 40 trees that date back to the time when the area was the Selangor Turf Club. The rest of the vegetation comprises indigenous species. There is also a jogging track, sculptures, a playground and children's wading pool (Tue–Fri 10am–7.30pm, Sat–Sun 10am–9.30pm). In the northeast corner stands the Uzbek-inspired **Masjid Asy-Syakirin** (Asy-Syakirin Mosque; daily 9am–9pm, except prayer times), featuring a metallic dome and delicate Islamic calligraphy.

In the southeast part of the KLCC is the Kuala Lumpur Convention Centre, where concerts and theatre performances are sometimes staged. Its concourse level is occupied by the **Aquaria KLCC** (www.aquariaklcc.com; daily 10am–8pm; last admission at 7pm). This family-oriented aquarium is stocked with over 5,000 fish and other marine life; it also has a rainforest exhibition.

Cheap tickets

Matinée tickets for the Malaysian Philharmonic Orchestra can go for as little as RM20. The programme also includes interesting and popular concerts for children.

NIGHTLIFE HUBS

The Petronas Twin Towers are surrounded by some of the best **nightlife** in Southeast Asia. The zigzagging streets of Jalan Sultan Ismail, Jalan P. Ramlee and Jalan Pinang are packed with clubs, pubs and restaurants

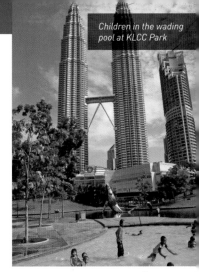
Children in the wading pool at KLCC Park

such as Poppy Collection, Rum Jungle, The Beach Club Café and that oldie-but-goodie, the Hard Rock Café. Meanwhile, Jalan Ampang's jewel is Zouk, which encases several clubs in an iconic egg-shaped structure. Jalan Doraisamy, west of KLCC, is home to the swanky Asian Heritage Row, a line of wonderfully renovated pre-war shophouses that are occupied by some of the fanciest eateries and watering holes in town.

KL TOWER

The **KL Tower** ② (Menara Kuala Lumpur; www.menarakl.com.my; daily 9am–10pm) is a scenic lookout offering a 360-degree view of the city. Located west of the Twin Towers on the Bukit Nanas hill, the KL Tower is, in fact, actually about 60m (197ft) taller than the former when measured from sea level because of its elevated location. Sporting a typical telecommunications tower design, the KL Tower comprises a huge shaft rising from the ground topped by a circular six-storey head, whose design is inspired by the traditional Malay spinning top *(gasing)*. The public **Observation Deck** is on the first level of the tower head and, weather permitting, is the best place to view the upper reaches of the Petronas Twin Towers, as well as the city. Binoculars and a good audio tour help enrich the visitor's viewing experience. The building also contains

A panoramic view of KL

souvenir shops, an amphitheatre, cafés and a revolving restaurant, Atmosphere360 (www.atmosphere360.com.my). Queues can be long during the school holidays.

The KL Tower has also been styling itself as an extreme sports venue. Two annual events draw a good crowd: the Kuala Lumpur International Towerthon Challenge (basically a run up the tower) and the Kuala Lumpur Tower International Jump, which involves BASE jumping (parachute-aided free-falling). Event dates are posted on the KL Tower website.

KL FOREST ECO PARK

The hill on which the KL Tower sits is the country's oldest forest reserve, gazetted in 1906 and purportedly the forest in which indigenous Orang Asli once hunted. The Orang Asli have long since moved out, and the reserve has been turned into the **KL Forest Eco Park** (formerly known as Bukit Nanas Forest Reserve; daily

7am–6pm). Despite being surrounded by concrete and glass, it is surprisingly lush and species-rich. Five short and well-marked trails have been developed, but visitors should check in first at the Forest Information Centre on Jalan Raja Chulan (daily 9am–5pm). There is also a herbal garden and an impressive canopy walkway. Be ready with insect repellent though.

In the western foothills of the Eco Park are two of Kuala Lumpur's best-achieving schools, housed in beautiful classical buildings. Built in English Gothic style, the all-girls **Convent Bukit Nanas** at the northern end of Jalan Bukit Nanas was established in 1899 by French Catholic nuns and was the city's first convent school. Its brother school down the road, **St John's Institution**, was established in 1904. Its main block is a brick-red Grecian-Spanish-influenced structure, among the most elaborate school buildings in KL.

Next to the boys' school is the dignified **St John's Cathedral** (www.stjohnkl.com.my; Mon–Fri 8.30am–1pm, 2–5pm, 2nd, 4th and 5th Sat of the month 8.30am–noon), which was built in 1883 and serves as the central Peninsular Malaysian Roman Catholic church. Built to originally serve expatriates and Eurasians, the church continues to draw an international parish and has a large Filipino congregation.

Down the hill from the cathedral and hugging the Lorong Ampang–Jalan Raja Chulan corner is the former **National Telecommunications Museum** (www.muziumtelekom.com.my; daily 9am–5pm). Now a telecommunications service point, the building is

Giant Jelutong

A magnificent century-old Jelutong tropical hardwood tree stands right by the KL Tower. During the tower's construction, a RM430,000 retaining wall was built around it to protect it.

On Jalan Bukit Bintang

one of the finest examples of neoclassical architecture in the city, complete with imposing columns and perfect proportions. It originally housed the Central Battery Manual Telephone Exchange.

Nearby is the Court Hill Ganesh Temple (Korttu Malai Pillayar; daily 8am–7pm) a beautiful Hindu temple from which the smell of incense constantly emanates. The temple is dedicated to Ganesh, the elephant-headed God and patron saint of, among other things, arts and sciences.

BUKIT BINTANG

Centred around **Jalan Bukit Bintang ㉑**, the Bukit Bintang area is packed with shopping centres, hotels, eateries and nightlife venues. Bukit Bintang (literally, 'Star Hill') was the undisputed centre of entertainment in 1950s Kuala Lumpur. However, over the years congestion, grime and vice set in, until 1999, when a visionary property mogul turned it around in a multi-million-Ringgit remodelling exercise. Other building owners soon followed suit, and today the entire area is vibrant and bustling. Topping the national per-square-metre density chart for commercial space, Bukit Bintang attracts a constant flow of bodies, from corporate types to the nouveaux riches. All malls open from 10am–10pm, with restaurants open till late.

BINTANG WALK

The masterstroke that saved Bukit Bintang from decrepitude is a promenade, 1km (0.6 miles), known as **Bintang Walk**, which runs from the Westin Hotel to the Lot 10 mall. Today, the walkway is so cluttered with sidewalk cafés, ice-creameries, shops and restaurants, it can hardly be seen.

Anchoring the Jalan Bukit Bintang at its northern end are two massive luxury malls. One is the David Rockwell, New York-designed **Starhill Gallery** (www.starhillgallery.com), which is linked to sister properties the J.W. Marriott Hotel and The Ritz-Carlton. It has dedicated product floors that are accessed in the lifts by their names rather than numbers. For example, the basement Feast Village features eateries galore, including a high-end hawker centre in a futuristic setting. Among the luxury branded stores are the Louis Vuitton and Sephora concept megastores, while a string of boutiques features highly specialised collectors' watches and jewellery.

In a face-off with Starhill is the newer **Pavilion Kuala Lumpur** (www.pavilion-kl.com), located opposite it. It, too, boasts exclusive local and international designer boutiques, restaurants and health and beauty stores. The difference is that these are sprawled over seven levels and almost 130,000 sq m (1.4 million sq ft) of

> ### Street parties
>
> Bukit Bintang frequently hosts street parties, when the roads are closed to traffic, and concerts and firework displays are staged. Occasions to look out for include New Year's Eve, Chinese New Year and the Sepang Formula One weekend. Check details with Tourism Malaysia.

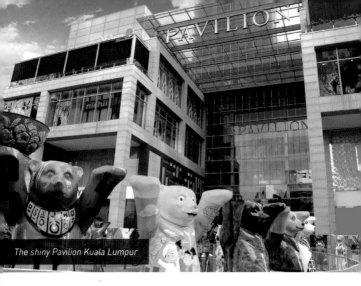
The shiny Pavilion Kuala Lumpur

street-front retail shops. Attractions include the Tokyo Street 'precinct', fashioned after Tokyo's Ginza and Shibuya shopping districts and containing an astounding variety of eateries. Pavilion is also in a 'self-contained' enclave comprising office blocks, residential towers and a luxury hotel.

There are two other shopping centres along Bintang Walk. **Fahrenheit 88** (www.fahrenheit88.com) is anchored by Japanese chain Uniqlo and houses innovative local couturier Bernard Chandran, who is also targeting the youth market with his Area27 multi-label store. The landmark green **Lot 10** (www.lot10.com.my) is a fashionable, upmarket hang-out whose main tenant is the Japanese-owned Isetan department store. It has a much-lauded food court where you can sample street food in air-conditioned comfort. On the rooftop is a cosy theatre run by The Actor's Studio (www.theactors studio.com.my).

ARAB SECTION

The shop lots next to the Pavilion, as well as a stretch along Jalan Sultan Ismail, are occupied by Arab restaurants offering a range of Middle Eastern cuisine. These restaurants have Moorish arches and tinkling fountains, as well as booths allowing women in *burqas* (burkas) to dine in private.

Since 2000, Muslim-friendly Malaysia has seen explosive growth in the number of Arab tourists. Malaysian hospitality to them starts at the Kuala Lumpur International Airport with services like announcements in Arabic and a special immigration lane for Arab tourists with families. The peak period for Middle Eastern tourists – mostly honeymooners and families – is from June to September.

SUNGEI WANG PLAZA AND BUKIT BINTANG PLAZA

Across the Jalan Sultan Ismail junction, bargain-hunters will appreciate the linked shopping centres of **Bukit Bintang Plaza** and **Sungei Wang Plaza**, whose entrance actually faces Jalan Sultan Ismail. Because most of the shops in these malls are small and their turnover quick, competition is stiff, which keeps prices low. Cool teenage gear is available at the Hong Kong station on Level 6 of Sungei Wang, while

Wooing shoppers

The presence of so many shopping centres in Kuala Lumpur means that competition among them is fierce. Therefore, events and promotions are becoming crucial in attracting customers. Shopping centres are especially fun to visit during the festive seasons of Chinese New Year, Hari Raya Puasa, Deepavali and Christmas, with innovative decorations, activities galore and seasonal goodies for sale. Meanwhile, the Mega Sale Carnival period from around June to September serves up some great bargains.

audiovisual equipment and cameras are good buys in the Bukit Bintang Plaza. The real draw of these shopping centres, though, is clothing, and the variety is mind-boggling, ranging from the latest hip-hop and East Asian fashion to quality Malaysian-made T-shirts and jeans. Accessories, shoes, cosmetics, toiletries and leather goods are also plentiful.

Perpendicular to Jalan Bukit Bintang on Jalan Imbi is **Berjaya Times Square**, whose products tend to be of lower quality. The mall also has a cineplex, IMAX theatre, bowling alley and an indoor theme park. Kuala Lumpur is also a great place to buy computers and computer accessories. Most shopping centres have an IT section, but the best buys are in the dedicated IT malls of **Low Yat Plaza** and **Imbi Plaza**.

JALAN CONLAY

While some Malaysian souvenirs are available for sale in Bukit Bintang, the place to go for a wide range of local products is a little bit away from the main shopping area. Northeast of Bukit Bintang along the quiet Jalan Conlay is the **Kuala Lumpur Craft Complex** ㉒ (Kompleks Kraf Kuala Lumpur; www.kraftangan. gov.my; daily 9am–7pm). This 'one-stop craft centre' – a more up-market version of the Central Market – has quality Malaysian arts and crafts for sale from all over the country, including basketry, textiles, silverware

Craft expo

Each year at the end of February/early March, in conjunction with National Craft Day, the Kuala Lumpur Craft Complex hosts a two-week festival of handicrafts from all over Malaysia. Visitors get the chance to speak to artisans, buy their products and see craft-making demonstrations. There are also cultural performances. For details, tel: 03-2162 7459.

An artist talks to a tourist at the Artists' Colony in the Craft Complex

and pottery. Visitors might also want to set aside a few hours to have a go at making their own batik artwork, pottery or woodcraft in its **Craft Village** (charge applies). In the **Artists' Colony** (daily 10am–6pm), established and up-and-coming Malaysian artists can be seen at their canvasses. They are generally open to having a chat and certainly to purchases.

Near this complex, at the junction of Jalan Stonor, is the **Heritage of Malaysia Trust** ㉓ (Badan Warisan Malaysia; www.badanwarisanmalaysia.org; Mon–Sat 10am–5pm). This nongovernmental organisation works mainly through advocacy and education towards the preservation and conservation of the country's architectural heritage. The Trust is housed in a 1925 colonial bungalow and has a small but excellent gift shop whose products range from books to cards and collectables. Visitors may also browse its resource centre (Tue–Sat 10am–4pm, by appointment).

Barbequing satay at a hawker stall

Not to be missed is a tour of the **Rumah Penghulu Abu Seman** (Mon–Sat 11am and 3pm), a beautiful traditional Malay house which sits in the Trust's grounds. An increasingly rare sight throughout the country, this all-timber house, formerly owned by a village headman, was relocated from the northern state of Kedah to Kuala Lumpur and restored by the organisation as an awareness-raising and conservation project.

JALAN ALOR AND CHANGKAT BUKIT BINTANG

One of the best places to sample local Chinese hawker food is **Jalan Alor** ㉔. Lined with eateries, this street's pavements are overtaken by a host of fluorescent-lit food stalls and rickety tables and stools come evening. You get the gamut of Chinese fare here, from simple noodle dishes to more adventurous foods like venison and tripe. Just walk along the street and stop when you see something that takes your fancy.

More good food is dished up at stalls along the parallel **Tengkat Tong Shin**, some of which have been around for decades. However, their continued existence cannot be guaranteed. The success of the main Jalan Bukit Bintang strip might have resuscitated commerce, but other consequences include rising rental costs and the influx of property investors keen on a piece of the pie. Subsequently, old families from this neighbourhood have been leaving the area. Many of the remaining pre-war houses along Tengkat Tong Shin have been turned into restaurants, pubs or 'flashpackers' – higher-end backpacker accommodation. This street has already become a centre for budget accommodation.

Meanwhile, trendy has really colonised the perpendicular **Changkat Bukit Bintang**. Watering holes and international restaurants are *de rigueur* here. Among local favourites are the Cuban salsa outfit Havana, the elegant Japanese jazz bar Yoko's, and the hot-and-happening party spot, Pisco Bar, which serves excellent cocktails. For great live local acts, check out No Black Tie on Jalan Mesui. Run by a classical pianist, this cosy club and restaurant was among the first to offer a performing space for upcoming singer-songwriters and remains a favourite among them.

DAY TRIPS

Kuala Lumpur is a great jumping off point for day trips. From museums and cave temples to lush forests and historic estuaries, the options are plentiful and varied. Many tourists find driving outside KL enjoyable, as the roads and highways are in good condition and go through interesting small towns and rural landscapes.

MUSEUM OF ASIAN ART AND RIMBA ILMU

Located in Kuala Lumpur's southwest corner, bordering Petaling Jaya, are two wonderful attractions within University Malaya, the oldest university in the country. The **Museum of Asian Art** ㉕ (Muzium Seni Asia; www.museum.um.edu.my; Mon–Thu 9am–1pm, 2–5pm, Fri 9am–12.15pm, 2.45–5pm) is a gem showcasing 6,000 pieces of art – mainly ceramics – spanning 4,000 years of history in Malaysia and Asia. Book ahead for a guided tour.

Rimba Ilmu ㉖ ('Forest of Knowledge') is a tropical botanical garden and one of the most important biological conservation centres in Malaysia (http://rimba.um.edu.my; Mon–Thu 9am–noon, 2–4pm, Fri 9am–noon, 2.45–4pm). It has an excellent interpretive exhibition on rainforests and the environment, a rainforest garden featuring five core collections, including medicinal plants, palms and citrus species, and, for guided tours only, the exquisite **Conservatory of Rare Plants and Orchids**, comprising 1,700 plants that are rare or are becoming rare, including begonias, orchids and giant 'umbrella leaf' palms.

SUNWAY LAGOON

Families love the **Sunway Lagoon** ㉗ (www.sunwaylagoon.com; daily 10am–6pm). Spread over 32 hectares (80 acres), it has five themed parks packed with rides and the world's largest man-made surf beach, complete with artificial waves. A great view of the park can be had from the **Sunway Pyramid** next door (daily 10am–10pm), an Egyptian-themed shopping centre anchored by a giant lion in a sphinx pose.

BATU CAVES

About half an hour's drive north of the city centre is the Sri Subramaniar Swamy, or **Batu Caves Temple** ㉘ (daily 6am–9pm), home to a cave temple halfway up a limestone massif. Hindu devotees started praying at this cave temple in 1891, when the only deity worshipped there was Murugan, represented by his vel (trident). Today that vel still sits in the **Temple Cave**, along with the

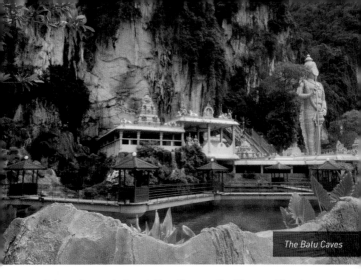

The Batu Caves

statues of several other deities. The cave itself is magnificent, an 80m by 100m (260ft by 330ft) chamber bedecked with stalactites and stalagmites, and opening at one end into a skylight.

These days, Murugan is also represented by a 43m (140ft) tall gilded **statue of Murugan**, the largest of its kind in the world. It stands at the bottom of the stairs to the Temple Cave. The rest of the temple complex comprises shrines to a host of other deities, including Ganesha, the elephant god, and Hanuman, the monkey god.

Batu Caves is particularly important for celebrants of the Hindu festival of repentance called **Thaipusam** at the end of January. A remarkable sensory experience, over a million devotees converge here to offer Murugan thanks and prayers, many offering acts of penance such as the carrying of large structures called *kavadi* or piercing their bodies with sharp spokes. The festival begins with the bearing of an important statue of Murugan here from the Sri Maha Mariamman Temple, a sister temple near Petaling Street.

FRIM

Tucked away in the hills northwest of Kuala Lumpur is one of the world's oldest forest research centres. The **Forest Research Institute of Malaysia** ㉙ (FRIM; www.frim.gov.my; daily 5am–7.30pm) is a showcase of tropical lowland vegetation spread over 600 hectares (1,480 acres). The One Stop Service Centre provides full details, as well as maps (daily 9am–5pm). FRIM's

---

⊘ RAINFOREST TOURS

At about 150 million years old, Malaysia's rainforests are among the world's oldest. They are also among the most diverse in species, with hundreds of thousands of flora and fauna identified and an unknown number still to be identified. Unfortunately, balancing environmental conservation and economic development is tricky, although the government is committed to sustainable development. Guided nature tours can give visitors a good understanding of the various rainforest ecosystems. The most common forest type in and around Kuala Lumpur is the dipterocarp forest. Dipterocarps are the most luxuriant of all plant communities, and comprise many timber species. Mangrove and other swamp forests are usually found in the lowlands, while the highest parts of the highlands are covered with montane forests. Large animals are difficult to sight in a forest, but smaller creatures are plentiful and fascinating. The best times for a jungle trek are in the early morning or late evening, when the forest creatures are liveliest. Trekkers should drink lots of water and wear sturdy walking shoes.

many attractions include six arboretums, including a world-renowned dipterocarp arboretum that contains some of the country's oldest and rarest trees. The main loop road brings you to most of them.

There are also five easy-walking nature trails that wind through the forest, ranging from 1–1.5km (0.6–1 mile). A sixth trail, the Rover Trail, climbs a steep hill and leads to FRIM's star attraction, the

Braving the FRIM Canopy Walkway

Canopy Walkway (Tue–Thu, Sat–Sun 9.30am–2.30pm; register and pay at the One Stop Service Centre, registration closes at 1.30pm; book ahead). This rope-and-ladder walkway, 200m (660ft) long, was built for scientists to study canopy-level flora and fauna, but visitors also get to appreciate it. The walkway is pretty high up – up to 30m (100ft) above the forest floor – and there are platforms along the way to take a breather and enjoy the view.

GENTING HIGHLANDS

Large, loud and kitschy define **Genting Highlands** ㉚ (www.rwgenting.com), the Las Vegas of Malaysia. An hour's drive northeast of Kuala Lumpur, Genting draws thousands to its hilltop attractions. From Gohtong Jaya halfway up the hill, the spectacular 3.4km (2-mile) **Genting Skyway Cable Car** glides silently above a carpet of montane vegetation (daily 7am–midnight).

At the top sprawl four hotels and apartments, all of which are interconnected. Follow the signs to get to the theme parks, three of which are indoors and one outdoors. All the hotels have sections of Malaysia's only legal casino (24 hours; age limit 21; dress code applies). In addition, two theatres feature local and international cabaret dinner shows, musicals and concerts.

KUALA GANDAH ELEPHANT CONSERVATION CENTRE

With the shrinking of natural forest cover, only 800–1,000 wild elephants are left in Peninsular Malaysia. Animals are increasingly feeding on crops and being chased off by planters. Individuals that cannot keep up with the herd, including babies and juveniles, are abandoned. As a result, the Department of Wildlife and National Parks set up the **Kuala Gandah National Elephant Conservation Centre** ③① (www.wildlife.gov.my; daily 10.30am–4pm) as a temporary base for elephants that need to be moved to protected areas or zoos. The centre is in Lanchang, 120km (75 miles) east of Kuala Lumpur.

Realising that education and awareness are key to conservation, the Department runs a visitor programme at the centre, where visitors get to know many interesting facts about the elephants. A documentary is screened

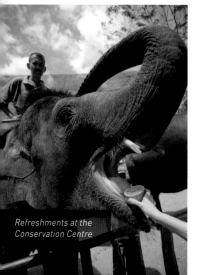

Refreshments at the Conservation Centre

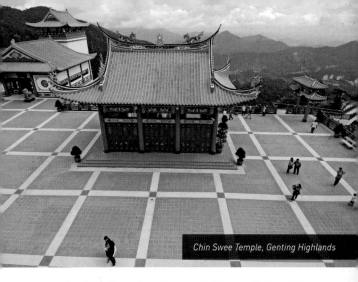

Chin Swee Temple, Genting Highlands

from Monday to Thursday at 1pm and 1.30pm, on Friday at 2pm and on Saturday, Sunday and public holidays at 12.30pm, 1pm and 1.30pm. At 2.15pm visitors can watch the elephants being given a bath by a mahout. Donations are welcome.

FRASER'S HILL

A real contrast to Genting Highlands is **Fraser's Hill** ㉜ (www.fraserhill.info), a peaceful hill resort whose attractions are its cool air and breathtaking mist-shrouded montane forest landscapes. Fraser's Hill is 104km (65 miles) north of Kuala Lumpur; the jump-off is the white-water-rafting centre of Kuala Kubu Bharu.

British Malaya's first hill station, the resort is named after an eccentric Englishman who ran a mule transport system and a gambling den for miners and planters. Many of the original 1900s grey-stone bungalows still stand. The town centre still has the original post office, police station and medical dispensary, but the landmark clock tower is a later addition. Visit the Information Centre located inside the Puncak Inn (tel: 09-5171 623; www.pkbf.gov.my; daily 8am–11pm) for a free map or to book guided nature walks or selected accommodation. The ring road around the golf course provides a pleasant two-hour stroll past old bungalows and newer resorts.

Visitors can take a refreshing dip in the **Jeriau waterfall**; note that the steps down are slippery after rain. With some of the richest birdlife in the peninsula, Fraser's Hill is a popular birdwatching destination. Nature-lovers should also explore the resort's eight jungle trails, but check trail conditions beforehand at the Information Centre. Break for Devonshire cream tea in the lovely garden of the colonial **Ye Olde Smokehouse** (daily 3–6pm).

The clock tower on Fraser Hill

KUALA SELANGOR

Standing at the estuary of the Selangor river, 67km (42 miles) from Kuala Lumpur, **Kuala Selangor** ㉝ was once a great capital whose past is partially preserved at **Bukit Melawati**. On this hill is a fort where many bloody battles were fought between the local sultans and the Dutch between 1778 and 1826. A 1.5km (1-mile) road brings you to the Dutch-built **Altingsburg**

Lighthouse (closed to visitors), opposite which is a **lookout** with views of the lush Kuala Selangor Nature Park. Peering over the lookout are six cannons from various periods of the war. Further along the walk are the remains of the **Melawati Gate**, the former gateway to the fort. Close-by is the **Royal Burial Ground** of the first three sultans of Selangor and their families. Entry

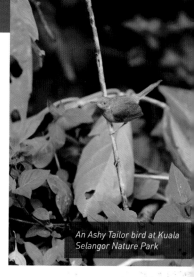

An Ashy Tailor bird at Kuala Selangor Nature Park

to the mausoleum is restricted, but visible through the gates is the sacred yellow cloth-covered cannon called the *Penggawa*, the sultan's most trusted protector.

At the foot of the hill, a road leads to fascinating mangrove forests of the **Kuala Selangor Nature Park** (Taman Alam Kuala Selangor; www.kuala-selangor.com; daily 9am–6pm), home to thousands of migratory water birds. Register first at the Visitors' Centre, which doubles as a gift shop. There are three trails of varying lengths; of note is the brackish lake at the end of the Egret Trail, where hundreds of herons congregate and breed.

When darkness descends, the magical firefly display at **Kampung Kuantan** ③④ begins. Between 7.30pm and 10.30pm, local villagers row visitors (four passengers per boat) past mangrove trees where millions of tiny male beetles flash synchronously; the flashing rate of three times a minute supposedly makes these the world's brightest fireflies.

Toy dragons for sale

WHAT TO DO

SHOPPING

While Kuala Lumpur is not in the same league as the shopping meccas of Singapore and Hong Kong, it does offer variety, quality and bargains. From international brands to Malaysian labels and handcrafted ethnic products, KL has something for every budget. What's more, with the increase in KL-ites' disposable income, 'masstige' brands – prestigious brands at affordable prices – have entered the market. The best bargains are during the annual nationwide Malaysia Mega Sale Carnival, which goes on for two months with prices slashed by up to 70 percent. Throughout the year, sales are also held by department stores. Sale periods can be crowded, so go early. Traffic can also be exceptionally bad, so use public transport.

SHOPPING MALLS

Shopping malls have become regular hang-outs for KL-ites, and the city just keeps building them, each one bigger than the last. Air-conditioned, they offer consumers not just shops but eateries, cinemas, exhibitions and even ice-skating rinks. Malls are anchored by department stores and supermarkets, as well as food courts, and goods for sale usually include clothes, household items, books, music, computers and audiovisual equipment. Photography and electronic goods are good buys.

The department stores and boutiques are the best places to buy well-made and affordable tropical-weather **clothes** and **shoes**, although very large sizes might be difficult to find. Among the home-grown labels are consumer brands Padini, Seed and Vincci, and the more up-market British India and Loewe;

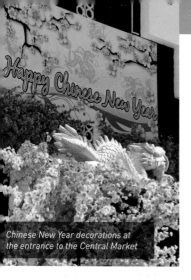

Chinese New Year decorations at the entrance to the Central Market

couturiers Zang Toi and Bernard Chandran have an international reputation.

During the major festivals of Chinese New Year, Hari Raya Puasa and Deepavali, there is an even greater variety of ethnic or ethnic-inspired clothing and accessories.

The main mall strip is at **Bukit Bintang** (see page 68), while **KLCC** has the high-end Suria KLCC and Avenue K. The **Mid-Valley** city near Brickfields houses the massive Mid-Valley Megamall and its up-market sister, The Gardens. North of this, in the classy suburb of **Bangsar**, are the luxury Bangsar Village I & II and the Bangsar Shopping Centre. **Petaling Jaya** is home to the Sunway Pyramid, as well as 1 Utama and The Curve.

SPECIALIST SHOPS

Move away from the malls and you will discover the cultural side of KL's shopping landscape.

Traditional fabrics are plentiful and both traditional designs and modern variations are available. The ever-popular **batik** is available in a range of fabrics, from cotton and voile to silk and satin. Choose from contemporary fashion as well as the usual sarongs, accessories, household and decorative items. *Songket*, the handwoven fabric with intricate tapestry inlaid with gold and metallic threads, appears in formal and ceremonial attire. It is also used as a handbag and shoe covering. From the Bornean state of Sarawak, woven *pua kumbu* textiles feature beautiful indigenous designs. Shop for these fabrics at Central Market and the Kuala Lumpur Craft Centre. Jalan Masjid India and Jalan Tuanku Abdul Rahman are great for songket and batik.

For textiles, head to the wholesale quarter of Jalan Tuanku Abdul Rahman, where you can also buy traditional Malay, Chinese and Indian outfits.

Gold jewellery is affordable and comes in contemporary or Malay-, Chinese- or Indian-influenced designs. Local goldsmiths use pure gold (up to 24-carat). Bargains can be found along Jalan Masjid India and Jalan Tuanku Abdul Rahman. **Kelantan silver** is fashioned into a variety of items, from brooches and costume jewellery to serving dishes and tableware, and is available in Central Market and the Kuala Lumpur Craft Centre. Malaysia's **pewterware** is renowned

⊘ THE ART OF BARGAINING

Prices are fixed in shopping malls and chain stores, but elsewhere, customers are expected to bargain. It is a bit of an act, but bargaining is also a great way to interact with locals. Being the first or last customer of the day usually gets you a good price, as does paying cash.

When you bargain, shop around so you know what the price range is. Especially in tourist areas, start by knocking 50 percent (or more) off the price, then increase the amount you are prepared to pay as the salesperson reduces their price. If you are not prepared to pay their 'final price', walk away; if your offer is within their profit range, they will call you back. If they do not, you know you have gone too low.

internationally for its stylish handmade designs. These can be found in malls and the Royal Selangor Pewter factory.

Malaysian and Asian **handicrafts** include bamboo and rattan products, traditional kites *(wau)*, pottery and Bornean beadwork. Shop for these at the Kuala Lumpur Craft Centre, Suria KLCC, Central Market and Peter Hoe. Fine wood-veneer souvenirs, including models of local buildings, are produced by Arch Collection at the KL City Gallery.

MARKETS AND GALLERIES

Cheap goods like T-shirts, jeans, leather products, and art and curios can be purchased at street markets like the **Petaling Street Bazaar** (which specialises in fake branded items – beware) and the **Jalan Melayu** market in the Masjid Jamek area.

The many different media and styles that make up Malaysian contemporary art make it a great souvenir and sometimes a good investment to boot. Tourist-targeted commercial artwork can be bought at the **Annexe**, Central Market (www.cmannexe.wordpress.com), while more expensive pieces by established and up-and-coming artists are available in art galleries throughout the city. Established names include Valentine Willie Fine Art, Galeri Taksu, Wei-Ling Gallery and Shalini Ganendra Fine Art, while collectives include Lost Generation Space and Matahati.

Night markets

Pasar malam, or night markets, are a great opportunity to experience local colour. Stalls are set up at around 6pm, and locals come to buy everything from fresh produce to underwear. Check out the pasar malam along Lorong Tuanku Abdul Rahman, off Jalan Masjid India (Sat), Jalan Berhala in Brickfields (Thu) and Jalan Maarof in Bangsar Baru (Sun).

The pool at SkyBar, Traders Hotel

ENTERTAINMENT

Kuala Lumpur has one of the hottest clubbing scenes in the region, with a plethora of venues ranging from warehouses to exclusive clubs, where international and local DJs spin a wide spectrum of house and other music, as well as live acts that feature commercial and more eclectic material. Watering holes are also plentiful and include specialist wine and cigar bars. The arts scene is smaller but active and reflects both Asian and Western influences in music, dance, theatre and the visual arts. For information on what's happening where, check newspapers, as well as magazines like *Juice* (www.juiceonline.com) and *Time Out* (www.timeoutkl.com). For arts write-ups and listings, go to *Kakiseni* (www.kakiseni.com).

NIGHTLIFE

Friday and Saturday nights are the best times to party in KL. KL-ites come out in full force, dressed up and ready to have fun. The action starts late, at around 11pm, and goes on until 2–3am. After this, do not be surprised to see clubbers head for a bite to eat. Live bands start their gigs at around 10pm. Clubs charge an entry fee from 10 or 11pm, which includes one drink. A good range of alcohol is stocked, but drinks are expensive, so do take advantage of happy hour, usually 5.30–9pm, when

Zouk's prime location

drinks are half-price; and ladies' nights, Wednesdays in most places, which offer free drinks for women. Beers start at RM12 a glass and RM50 a jug, spirits at RM18, and wine at RM25 a glass and RM80 a bottle. You can keep a tab going until you leave. Waiters generally expect a tip.

KL-ites tend to dress up to go to the fancier clubs, and some places do enforce dress codes, which for men stipulate, at the minimum, a collared T-shirt, long trousers and covered shoes; other places have a 'no jeans, shorts and sandals' rule. Most clubs adhere to the 21-year-old minimum age (the legal drinking age) and in clubs patronised mainly by Muslims, little alcohol is consumed.

Clubs are gay-friendly and nightlife choices for the gay community abound, although they are not openly advertised because of secular and religious laws.

Clubs

Head for the entertainment clusters, which feature multi-outlet complexes comprising at least one club, a chill-out bar and a restaurant. **Jalan P Ramlee**, near the KLCC, features giants like **The Beach Club Café** and **Thai Club & Bistro**. Nearby at 12 Jalan Pinang is the ultra-hip **Kyo Club Malaysia** (www.clubkyokl.com). Where upbeat is concerned, the Jalan Doraisamy area continues to reign with **Asian Heritage Row** establishments like the glitzy

Main Room KL. Changkat Bukit Bintang's gems are **Uptown Dance Bar** (No. 14&15) and **Havana Club**. Russian splendour-inspired **Rootz Dance Club**, at Lot 10 mall's rooftop, predominates in Bukit Bintang. Most good hotels have clubs as standard fixtures; notable outfits are Kuala Lumpur Hilton's exclusive **Zeta Bar** and Traders Hotel's luxurious **SkyBar**. Another popular option along Jalan Tun Razak is **Zouk Club** (www.zoukclub.com.my).

Live music

Live jazz can be enjoyed at **Yoko's** (36 Changkat Bukit Bintang), **No Black Tie** (17 Jalan Mesui; www.noblacktie.com.my), **Alexis Bistro Ampang** (Great Eastern Mall, 303 Jalan Ampang) and **Upstairs Alexis Telawi** (29A Jalan Telawi 3, Bangsar; both at www.alexis. com.my). No Black Tie and the two Alexis venues are also among the best places to catch gigs by local musicians and songwriters.

Mainstream bands perform regularly at **Hard Rock Café** (Concorde Hotel), while popular venues for underground music are the **Annexe** (Central Market; www.cmannexe.wordpress. com), **The One Café** (Jalan Tunku Abdul Rahman) and **MCPA Hall** (Chinese Assembly Hall). Hotel lounges usually feature good Filipino bands playing covers.

Pubs and bars

Good hotels have lounges or bars where you can wind down with a drink, and these vary from the luxurious **Luna Bar** at the Pacific Regency Hotel Suites (www.pacific-regency.com), with its breathtaking views, to the trendsetting Tujo Bar-serrie & Grill (www.tujo.my) at Ascott Hotel, which centres around the concept of a Playground.

Like clubs, watering holes are clustered in the entertainment areas. Bukit Bintang features the up-market choices of Starhill Gallery and Pavilion; Changkat Bukit Bintang's pubs in pre-war shophouses are always packed; Suria KLCC has its esplanade-facing outlets, while Jalan Doraisamy has its glamorous Asian Heritage Row hang-outs. Outside the city centre, Bangsar watering holes attract the beautiful people, while other favourite chill-out places are the Petaling Jaya enclaves of Sri Hartamas and Mont Kiara.

THE ARTS

Traditional Malay performances of dance, music and theatre have been relegated to mainly tourist events, with the only regular showcases being at the Malaysia Tourism Centre (Jalan Ampang; www.matic.gov.my) and Central Market (Jalan Hang Kasturi; www.centralmarket.com.my).

The **classical Indian dance** movement is very active. The key exponents are the Sutra Dance Theatre (www.sutrafoundation.org.my) and the Temple of Fine Arts (www.tfa.org.my). **Traditional Chinese performances** are not staged regularly, although Chinese orchestra Dama (www.dama.asia) is

⊘ INDEPENDENT FILMS

Thanks to digital video, Malaysian film-makers have been carving an international reputation for producing award-winning short films. Names to look out for are Amir Muhammad, Tan Chui Mui and Namewee.

Check listings for short-film and indie festivals such as the Freedom Film Festival and screenings by the film club Kelab Seni Filem Malaysia. Screenings are usually held at the Annexe (Central Market), Help University College (Petaling Jaya), MAPKL at Publika (Hartamas) and the Kuala Lumpur Performing Arts Centre (Sentul).

one name to look out for. Chinese opera is performed only during the Hungry Ghost Festival.

Contemporary performances of theatre and dance are staged regularly and draw from both Western and local traditions. Venues for these are KLPAC, the Annexe Central Market (www.cmannexe.wordpress.com), MAPKL at Publika, Solaris Dutamas, The Actors Studio @ Lot 10 (www.theactorsstudio.com.my) and Istana Budaya (www.istanabudaya.gov.my); Istana tends to feature large-scale musicals.

Performers in traditional costume

The **Petronas Philharmonic Hall** (Petronas Twin Towers; www.mpo.com.my) has a good, year-round classical music programme.

For **visual arts**, new galleries are opening all the time, including alternative art spaces. Check out local artists' work at venues like the National Visual Arts Gallery (see page 48), Petronas Art Gallery (Suria KLCC), Islamic Arts Museum Malaysia (see page 53), Valentine Willie Fine Art (Bangsar), Gallery Taksu (Jalan Pawang; http://taksu.com), Wei-Ling Gallery (Brickfields; www.weiling-gallery.com) and NN Gallery (Ampang; www.nngallery.com.my).

CINEMAS

KL's cinemas attract a steady clientele. Located in malls, local cinemas are state-of-the-art, air-conditioned and cheap, with some chains offering 3D, IMAX and luxury halls. Choose from mainstream Hollywood, Bollywood and Hong Kong cinema, with a scattering of local Malay-language films, Southeast Asian movies and arthouse releases. Blockbusters often get released on the same day as in the US, UK or Hong Kong, and queues can be long.

Non-Malay-language movies have Bahasa Malaysia and Mandarin subtitles, and censorship can sometimes be irritating.

SPORTS

SPECTATOR SPORTS

Malaysians are mad about **football**, which they call *bola*, whether it's the English Premier League or the Malaysia Cup. Fans dress up in club colours and get quite excited during live matches, whether at stadia or live television broadcasts at pubs and 24-hour *mamak* centres. **Formula One** fans flock to the Sepang International Circuit each year to watch motorsport's premier race and the annual **KL International Tower Jump** draws crowds as BASE jumpers defy death from the top of the KL Tower.

PARTICIPANT SPORTS

Hotels with a four-star rating and above have swimming pools and gym facilities or fitness centres; often these offer yoga, aerobics or pilates classes as well. There are special sprung **jogging trails** at the Lake Gardens and KLCC Park. Runners should also contact the Kuala Lumpur Hash House Harriers (www.motherhash.com), a running and beer-drinking group with roots in colonial times, which conducts family-oriented fun runs all over the city.

Good hotels should be able to arrange **golf** sessions. KL is surrounded by good golf courses, with at least 50 within an hour's drive of the city. Visitors have to pay green fees (RM80–400) and produce handicap cards. For details, contact the Malaysian Golfing Association (www.mgaonline.com.my).

Bowling enthusiasts might like the facilities and long opening hours at the state-of-the-art 38-lane Cosmic Bowl (Mid-Valley Megamall) and 48-lane Pyramid Megalanes (Sunway Pyramid), where the national bowling team trains.

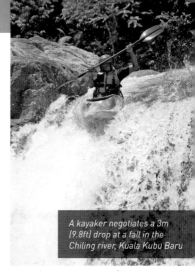

A kayaker negotiates a 3m (9.8ft) drop at a fall in the Chiling river, Kuala Kubu Baru

NATURE-BASED ACTIVITIES

Many of the places that make great day trips (see page 75) offer opportunities to try nature-based and adventure sports. The special interest groups of the Malaysian Nature Society (www.mns.my) also organise various activities. **Jungle trekking** is the best way to experience the natural beauty of the country. Always check in first with information centres or park authorities, dress adequately, carry enough water and bring insect repellent. **White-water sports** are popular in Kuala Kubu Bharu, the jump-off for Fraser's Hill. Have a go at rafting, canoeing or tubing (floating down a stream on a rubber tube).

For **caving**, guided nature tours of a limestone cave ecosystem are conducted at the Dark Caves. Choose from a 20-minute or hour-long nature tour or the three- to four-hour-long adventure-caving tour. For licensed operators, see page 121. **Mountain biking** has a good following. Clubs such as the

Spas

KL's best spas and spa treatments are in hotels, although day centres are improving. Visitors to the city will find a choice of international spa chains, beautifully designed venues and attractive packages for different budgets. These packages range from hour-long treatments to hotel spa holidays that combine a wide variety of recreational activities with treatments.

Pedalholics Cycling Club and the Kuala Lumpur Mountain Bike Hash organise short and long-distance rides.

CHILDREN'S KUALA LUMPUR

Kuala Lumpur has fun activities for children of all ages, although it is not very baby-friendly, as facilities for breastfeeding and nappy-changing, as well as push-chairs, are inadequate.

The best children's activity in town is the interactive science discovery centre **Petrosains** (see page 63), at Suria KLCC, whose innovative displays provide hours of fun and learning. Also at KLCC, the **Petronas Philharmonic Hall** holds family fun days.

The **School of Hard Knocks**, at the Royal Selangor Pewter Factory in Setapak Jaya (bookings compulsory; http://visitorcentre.royalselangor.com), offers children the chance to create their own pewter masterpieces with a few simple tools. Batik, pottery and woodcraft workshops are held at the **Kuala Lumpur Craft Complex** (see page 72).

The **Sunway Lagoon Water Theme Park** (see page 76) has great rides, plus the world's largest man-made surf beach. There are large children's playgrounds at the **KLCC Park** and the **Lake Gardens**. The former also has a wading pool. The latter offers a host of wildlife experiences at the Bird Park, Butterfly Park and Deer Park.

CALENDAR OF EVENTS

Many festival dates are not fixed as they follow the lunar and Muslim calendars. Check exact dates with Tourism Malaysia (www.tourism.gov.my).

January/February: *Thaipusam*: the festival of repentance, celebrated by Hindus bearing milk pots and *kavadi* structures at the holy shrine at Batu Caves; *Federal Territory Day* (1 Feb): parades and other events in celebration of Kuala Lumpur's birthday; *Chinese New Year*: the start of the lunar year is celebrated with festive goodies and decorations.

March: *National Craft Day*: week-long festival of handicrafts from all over Malaysia at the Kuala Lumpur Craft Complex; *Malaysian Formula One Grand Prix*: Formula One action at the Sepang International Circuit.

May: *Wesak Day*: devotees offer prayers and give alms to monks in Buddhist temples to commemorate Buddha's birth, enlightenment and death; *Colours of Malaysia (Citrawarna)*: a colourful festival showcasing Malaysia's cultural diversity, kicked off by an extravagant parade along Jalan P Ramlee.

June: *Malaysia Mega Sale Carnival* (Jun–Sep): huge country-wide sale.

July/August: *National Day* (31 Aug): Independence from British colonial rule is marked with much putting up of flags; state capital cities take turns to host parades and concerts.

September: *Festival of the Hungry Ghosts*: Chinese street concerts staged to appease the spirits of the dead; *Mooncake Festival*: this mid-Autumn festival is celebrated with mooncakes and colourful lanterns; *Malaysia Day* (16th) marks the day Sabah and Sarawak joined Malaya to form Malaysia.

October/November: *Deepavali*: the Hindu Festival of Lights is marked by prayers and celebrations. Brickfields is particularly exciting.

December: *Christmas* (25 Dec): festive decor and carolling in malls, and midnight church masses; *New Year's Eve* (31 Dec): concerts, countdowns and fireworks in Bukit Bintang and KLCC.

Variable dates: *Hari Raya Puasa*: the city is painted green as Muslims usher in the end of the Ramadan fasting month with prayers, feasts and visits to friends and family; during Ramadan, special bazaars spring up all over the city; *Hari Raya Haji*: this Muslim festival marking the *haj* (pilgrimage to Mecca) is observed with prayers and feasts.

EATING OUT

From the fragrant brown cinnamon bark to the sour pulp of the tamarind, the spicy flower buds of cloves to the pungent rhizome of the galangal, it was the spices of the Malay lands that spurred trade, fuelled the rise and fall of empires, and influenced the world's gastronomy. These aromatic products attracted a host of peoples to the Malay Archipelago, who, in turn, brought ingredients, cooking styles and food from their own lands. At the same time, the mixing of these peoples through the ages saw the hybridisation and enriching of tastes, textures and flavour. The result is contemporary Malaysian food, astonishing in its variety and uniqueness.

Kuala Lumpur offers all of the regional Peninsula specialities, from the sour and spicy northern dishes to the creamy curries of the south and the fish specialities of the east coast. Though not as widespread, Bornean specialities such as noodle dishes can also be found. With increased incomes and globalisation, the number of chic bistros and fine-dining restaurants has increased and other Asian and Continental fare is now served.

Smoking allowed

Although smoking is officially not allowed in enclosed restaurants, the rule is ignored in mamak outfits almost all the time, and in some bistros and cafés, with 'smoking' tables placed near the entrance.

Innovations abound, from entire cuisines such as Nonya food to Chinese-style stir-fried vegetables served alongside Indian curries. Nonetheless, it is hawker food that arguably tops the taste chart, simple wholesome fare from age-old recipes dished up in no-frills coffee shops and roadside stalls. The plenitude of eating places is due to Malaysians' great fondness for eating out. Because it is affordable and convenient, eating out daily for lunch and even dinner is normal.

Outlets can be crowded during weekends and holidays, especially child-friendly eateries and new restaurants.

Below are the main cuisines found in KL, described in broad strokes and including a few staples. The main meal across all local cuisines comprises rice served with several meat and vegetable dishes, which are shared communally.

Breakfast at a Chinese coffee shop on Petaling Street

MALAY CUISINE

The fresh, aromatic spices of the land, combined with herbs from India, the Middle East and China, are what define the spicy and robust flavours of Malay food. The cuisine traditionally features rice, fish, fresh vegetables and the chilli-based *sambal* (a type of relish, often made with *belacan* shrimp paste). Food is always seasoned with spices, and coconut milk and the sour tamarind juice are important ingredients.

The most recognisable concoction to foreigners is probably satay, marinated and charcoal-grilled skewered chicken, beef or mutton; it is served with a thick, spicy peanut sauce. The day for many Malaysians usually starts with *nasi lemak*, rice cooked in coconut milk served with condiments like peanuts, fried anchovies, cucumber, egg and a *sambal*. Common lunch and dinner dishes are *ayam masak merah*, a piquant chicken dish cooked with tomatoes and chillies; *rendang*, a dry beef or chicken curry; and *ikan bakar*, fish wrapped in a banana leaf and charcoal-grilled. Salads are also popular, eaten raw (*ulam*) or in a spicy mix (*kerabu*). Malay food also includes a large variety of *kuih* (cakes), featuring coconut, glutinous rice, bananas or palm sugar.

CHINESE CUISINE

Most Malaysian Chinese cuisine features the southern regional styles of China, from where early migrants originated. Food

⊙ FUSION FARE

The word in trendy dining among KL's chichi set is fusion fare; generally a mix of Eastern and Western ingredients and cooking styles. However, with so much good traditional food available – and the organic evolution of the traditional Nonya and Eurasian fusion cuisines – purists tend to dismiss contemporary fusion fare as faddish, presentation-focused or an excuse for exorbitant pricing in the name of novelty.

The counter argument to this is that because there is so much good traditional food, local and international chefs have a huge palette with which to experiment. Today, all sorts of fusion fare is available, with the best including the contemporary French cuisine of Cantaloupe at Troika Sky Dining, the innovative Cantonese offerings at Celestial Court at Sheraton Imperial Hotel, the Japanese-infused preparations of Hotel Maya's Still Waters *sosaku* restaurant, the exquisite Cilantro in the Micasa All Suite Hotel and the amazing rooftop restaurant at Impiana KLCC Hotel, Cedar on 15.

is stir-fried, steamed or deep-fried, and meat dishes, soups and noodles are occasionally infused with local elements like black pepper, curry leaves and *sambal*.

A quintessentially KL dish is the hawker preparation of Hokkien *mee*, thick yellow wheat noodles fried in dark soy sauce with pork and prawns. Another Hokkien favourite is *bak kut teh*, a fragrant herbal soup of pork ribs. From the

Different satay skewers at a hawker food stall

Cantonese come such favourites as *char siu* (barbecued pork) and refined multi-course banquets. *Dim sum* is a feast in itself, with numerous varieties of steamed, fried or baked dumplings and more.

Many Hainanese immigrants operate *kopitiam,* or coffee shops, which serve the perennial favourite, Hainanese chicken rice, as well as noodles and good tea and coffee. The Hainanese were also favoured as cooks for the colonials, resulting in Chinese variations of chicken chop and pork chop. *Teochew* porridge is a popular supper option, where plain rice broth is eaten with salty, preserved food, as well as richer fare like braised goose. The Hakkas created *yong tau fu*, an assortment of bean curd and vegetables stuffed with fish and meat paste.

Chinese hawker fare from the northern Malaysian state of Penang is the most famous and, some argue, the tastiest; must-tries include *char kway teow*, stir-fried flat noodles with prawns and bean-sprouts, and Hokkien prawn *mee*, featuring noodles in a light, spicy pork-flavoured soup. Sarawak laksa is a popular creamy coconut noodle dish.

INDIAN CUISINE

Because of its dominance in the culinary landscape, piquant Tamil cuisine, typified by breads and 'banana leaf rice' meals, has become synonymous with 'Indian food' in Malaysia. The former comprises griddled breads like *roti canai* and *thosai* accompanied by the lentil *dhal* dish or a curry. Like the Malay *nasi lemak*, *roti canai* has become a favourite breakfast dish of all Malaysians.

Ordering 'banana leaf rice' will see a banana leaf placed before you on which hot rice is heaped along with three different vegetables and a choice of chicken or beef curries – usually a dry *varuval* or coconut-milk-laced perutal curry – or fried fish. These eateries also serve good vegetarian meals.

Meanwhile, 24-hour Indian-Muslim, or *mamak,* eateries serve spicier *halal* South Indian food. This has roots in Penang's *nasi kandar*, named after the way early Indian-Muslim hawkers used to carry rice *(nasi)* and curry in two baskets balanced on a *kandar*, or pole. Traditional *nasi kandar* curries include fish-head curry – a local concoction – and tiger-prawn masala. Some of these *mamak* serve the North Indian tandoori favourites and *biryani* rice, too.

North Indian restaurants are higher-end, and KL-ites tend to gravitate towards the tandoori and *naan* bread sets,

Malaysian cutlery

Malaysians generally eat rice meals with a fork and spoon (spoon in the right hand). Malays and Indians use their fingers (right hand only; the left hand is considered unclean), while Chinese food is usually eaten with chopsticks.

although a wide variety of food is available. Certainly, the finer dishes of the maharajahs are available in sumptuously appointed restaurants, complete with live music.

NONYA CUISINE

Nonya food, also called Peranakan or Straits Chinese food, is a delicious hybrid of Malay and Chinese cuisines that evolved over centuries and is largely flavoured by well-blended,

An Indian sweets vendor

complex spice pastes. The cuisine took root in the 15th century when traders from China started settling down in the Malay Peninsula, marrying locals and adopting local customs.

A lovely starter is *pai ti* (also known as top hats), a savoury bean, shrimp or pork and carrot mixture served in a delicate pastry shell. Dishes like *kari kapitan* (a coconut-based chicken curry), *lemak nenas* (pineapple curry) and *buah keluak kay* (chicken braised with mangrove nuts) are more Malay in character, while dishes like *loh bak* (meat rolls) and *hong bak* (pork braised in spices and bean paste) are decidedly more Chinese. No Nonya meal is complete without *sambal belacan* (chilli and dried-shrimp paste) and a dash of lime.

Laksa, a soupy noodle dish, comes in two versions: curry *laksa* has a rich red gravy with a coconut milk base, while *asam laksa* has a fish-based sour, tangy soup.

Like the Malays, the Nonyas are also famous for their pains-takingly prepared desserts, such as *pulut tai tai* (sticky blue-and-white rice cakes) served with *kaya* (coconut egg jam) and the Chinese New Year speciality of *kuih kapek*, crispy folded biscuits.

OTHER CUISINES

While cuisines from the rest of the world have long been part of KL's dining scene, they have assumed a wider and more sophisticated flavour recently. Continental, Mediterranean, Mexican and Middle Eastern restaurants have become part of local choices, as have Japanese, Korean, Thai and Indochinese ones. Besides the downtown entertainment clusters, many eateries are located near embassies or expatriate enclaves in the up-market sections of Jalan Ampang and Bangsar.

DRINKS

Tea and coffee are copiously drunk in KL, and a range of preparations is available, so be specific when ordering. Among local favourites is *teh tarik*. Made of tea powder, condensed milk and evaporated milk, this 'pulled tea' is prepared by repeatedly pouring it from a glass held high into another held below. This creates a thick froth, cools down the tea and ensures a thorough mix. This art can be witnessed in coffee shops, but there are even national-level *teh tarik*-making competitions. American coffee-shop chains such as Starbucks and San Francisco are plentiful and popular, likewise local chains based on traditional *kopitiam*. Chinese tea is drunk with Chinese food, although in *kopitiam* herbal variations are popular, too.

KL-ites sometimes order just a glass of warm water to go with their meal; this is generally boiled water from the tap, but mineral water is also available. Ice cubes are generally safe to consume in large restaurants.

Muslims are not permitted by their religion to drink alcohol, and it is therefore generally not available in Muslim eateries. However, elsewhere alcohol can easily be ordered, with beer and stout being the most popular, even in Chinese *kopitiam*. Wine is also popular, especially table wines and New World varieties, and a wide range, including high-quality labels, is available in the restaurants, clubs and wine and cigar bars patronised by discerning KL-ites. However, alcohol is extremely expensive, so KL-ites take full advantage of happy hour two-for-the-price-of-one deals.

TO HELP YOU ORDER...

You can use English to order your food in restaurants, but Bahasa Malaysia is useful at hawker stalls and *mamak* shops.

Do you have...? **Ada tak... ?**
I'd like this/that. **Saya mahu ini/itu.**
I don't want this/that. **Saya tidak mahu ini/itu.**
I eat only vegetarian food. **Saya hanya makan makanan sayuran.**
I can eat spicy food. **Saya boleh makan makanan pedas.**
Not spicy. **Tidak pedas.**
The bill, please. **Tolong beri saya bil.**

a little **sedikit**	vegetables **sayur**
a lot **banyak**	rice **nasi**
bread **roti**	coffee with/without milk **kopi/kopi o**
egg noodles **mee**	
vermicelli **meehoon**	iced coffee **kopi ais**
flat noodles **kway teow**	tea with/without milk **teh/teh o**
ice **ais**	
beef **daging**	Chinese tea **teh Cina**
fish **ikan**	beer **bir**
pork **babi**	iced water **ais kosong**

PLACES TO EAT

The price symbols below are intended as a guide and are based on a standard meal for two, without drinks.

$$$$	over RM90
$$$	RM60–90
$$	RM30–60
$	under RM30

AROUND DATARAN MERDEKA

The Canteen by Chef Adu $ *National Textiles Museum, 26 Jalan Sultan Hishamuddin; tel: 03-2694 3457.* This cute museum café offers Asian fusion cuisine and is curated by one of Malaysian MasterChef's judges, Chef Adu Amran Hassan. Open daily 9am–6pm.

Kafe Old Market Square $ *2 Medan Pasar, tel: 03-2022 2338;* http://cafe oldmarketsquare.com. This Hainanese coffee shop in the oldest part of Yap Ah Loy's Chinatown replaced the old Sin Seng Nam restaurant, which had been in business for 85 years. The new place keeps its predecessor's original fittings and menus. Try its delicious Hainanese chicken rice, curried chicken or stir-fried noodles. A traditional breakfast of toast with *kaya* (coconut jam), half-boiled egg and coffee is also served. Open Mon–Fri 7am–6pm, Sat 7am–3pm.

Precious Old China Restaurant and Bar $$ *Lot 2, Mezzanine floor, Central Market; tel: 03-2273 7372;* www.oldchina.com.my. Vietnamese deities, Victorian furniture and Chinese antique wall panels decorate this Nonya restaurant. Traditional recipes are superbly executed, with complex spices infusing the meats, and the curries are nicely rich. Do not miss dessert. Open daily 11.30am–10pm.

Restoran Yusoof dan Zakhir $ *42, 44, 46 Jalan Hang Kasturi; tel: 03-2026 8685.* Enjoy *nasi kandar* clay-pot staples such as curried prawns and spicy lamb korma in this popular eatery opposite the Central Market. It also has excellent breakfast choices such as *apam* pancakes and *idly* and *puri* breads. Wash it down with a tea or fresh coconut. Open daily 6am–11pm.

PETALING STREET

Hong Ngek Restaurant $ *50 Jalan Tun H.S. Lee; tel: 03-2078 7852.* Located near Jalan Tun Perak, this gem of a Chinese restaurant dates back to the 1940s. Hokkien-style Chinese food is served here, a speciality being pomfret cooked in two styles: deep-fried and steamed. The Hokkien *mee* is excellent and it is also worth trying the oyster omelette. Open Mon–Fri 11am–5pm, Sat 10.30am–5pm, closed Sun and public holidays.

Old China Café $$ *11 Jalan Balai Polis; tel: 03-2072 5915;* www.oldchina. com.my. The best time-trip café in KL, the old-world ambience, memorabilia and marble-topped tables here provide the perfect location for memorable Nonya cuisine. Specialities include *laksa* (noodles in spicy gravy) and fish head in tamarind sauce. Try the delicious sago dessert called *gula melaka*. Open 11.30am–10pm.

Peter Hoe Beyond $ *62-1 first floor, The Row, Jalan Doraisamy; tel: 18-223 5199.* Simple, wholesome fare is the order of the day at this tiny, chic café located within a terrific boutique. Munch on quiches, pies and salads, or, if it is teatime, lemon pies and cupcakes. Open daily 10am–7pm.

Soong Kee Beef Noodles $ *86 Jalan Tun H.S. Lee; tel: 03-2078 1484.* This hole-in-a-wall eatery with just a handful of tables and chairs at the corner of Jalan H.S. Lee has been making the best beef dumplings in the city for seven decades. Enjoy them in a soup accompanied by fine springy egg noodles in a dark sauce with minced pork and garlic. Open Mon–Sat 11am–10.30pm, closed Sun and public holidays.

JALAN MASJID INDIA AND KAMPUNG BARU

Coliseum Café $ *98–100 Jalan Tuanku Abdul Rahman; tel: 03-2692 6270;* www.coliseum1921.com. Get whisked back to the British colonial days in this café. Guzzle down a gunner (a mix of ginger ale, ginger beer and bitters), then embark on a sizzling rib-eye steak or a baked crabmeat salad and fried prawn fritters with tartare sauce. The English pot pies here are still baked in a firewood oven. Open daily 10am–10pm.

Nasi Kandar Kudu bin Abdul $ *335 Jalan Tunku Abdul Rahman; tel: 016-287 2123*. Spice lovers will enjoy this popular no-frills Penang *nasi kandar* eatery, located across from Centrepoint Hotel. The curries here feature seafood, including creamy fish roe, as well as chunky chicken and mutton; a speciality here is the *ayam sambal bawang* (chicken in an onion and chilli paste). Lunch-time queues can be long. Open Mon–Sat 7.30am–8pm.

Nasi Lemak Wanjor Kampung Baru $ *8 Jalan Raja Muda Musa; tel: 012-395 3884*. Queue up for one of KL's best preparations of Malaysia's favourite breakfast, *nasi lemak*. Have your fluffy, steamed rice with a simple, sweetish anchovy *sambal* (chilli paste) and hard-boiled egg, or add squid, beef *rendang* or curried chicken. Wash it down with a hot local tea or coffee. Open daily 6.30am–noon, 3pm–1am.

Pasar Minggu $ *Jalan Raja Muda Musa*. This is a no-frills hawker centre right where Jalan Raja Alang meets Jalan Raja Muda Musa. Stall number GSA14 serves delicious Javanese *lontong*, a soupy compressed-rice and vegetable dish where the rice roll is steamed in a banana leaf, and GSA13 serves the hard-to-find *kuih lopis*, a triangular glutinous rice dessert coated in desiccated coconut and served with palm sugar. Open daily 7am–noon.

Saravanaa Bhavan $ *1007 Selangor Mansion, Jalan Masjid India; tel: 03-2698 3293;* www.saravanabhavan.com. Delicious Indian vegetarian fare is served in this chain restaurant. An extensive menu offers everything from breads to rice, and even Chinese Indian preparations. The set meals are good value and the sweets are delectable and good with masala tea or Bru coffee. There are also outlets in Bangsar and Petaling Jaya. Open daily 8am–10.30pm.

Yut Kee $ *Jalan Kamunting, off Jalan Dang Wangi; tel: 03-2698 8108*. A popular, atmospheric Hainanese coffee shop dating back to the 1920s, Yut Kee is well known for *roti babi*, a sandwich filled with minced pork and crabmeat, dipped in egg and deep-fried and served with Worcestershire sauce. Another must-try is the Swiss roll with *kaya* (coconut jam). An assortment of noodles is also available. Open Tue–Sun 7.30am–4.30pm.

LAKE GARDENS AND BRICKFIELDS

Restaurant Chat Masala $ *259G Jalan Tun Sambanthan, Brickfields; tel: 03-2260 3244.* The constant Indian vegetarian crowd is testament to this eatery's consistent standards. Located near the Jalan Berhala junction, the chefs dish up tasty snacks (*chaat*) such as crispy *puri* bread variations, as well as vegetarian meat-substitute favourites like mutton *varuval* and chicken masala. Open daily 7.30am–11.30pm.

Restoran Rebung Dato Chef Ismail $$ *1 Jalan Tanglin, Taman Botani Perdana; tel: 03-2276 3535;* www.restoranrebungdatochefismail.com. The emphasis at this popular restaurant is on the preservation of Malay culinary heritage through buffet style dinners and lunches. There is also an option to sample a taste of the colonial with their excellent hi-teas. Open daily 7am–10pm.

Vishal Food and Catering $ *22 Jalan Scott, Brickfields; tel: 03-2274 0995.* Opposite the Hanuman temples, this simple Chettiar family-run restaurant serves excellent traditional meals that are subtle blends of sweet, sour and lightly spicy. A typical set is rice with *sambar* (stew made from pulses) and *puli kulambu* (tamarind curry); end with sweet *payasam* (pudding). Open daily 7am–11pm.

KLCC

Ciao Ristorante $$$ *20A Jalan Kampung Pandan, off Jalan Tun Razak; tel: 03-9285 4827;* www.ciao.com.my. Located in a gorgeous bungalow behind the Royal Selangor Golf Club, this well-established Italian restaurant uses quality ingredients to make straightforward tasty meals. The menu ranges from fresh pasta dishes and pizzas to succulent lamb. The set lunches are good value. Open Mon–Fri 12–2.30pm, daily 6–10.30pm.

Elegant Inn $$$ *2.01 Level 2, Menara Hap Seng, Jalan P Ramlee; tel: 03-2070 9399.* With a spacious dining hall and some private dining rooms, this refined restaurant is located on the 2nd floor of Menara Hap Seng. Come for the outstanding dim sum this place is famous for and some other Chinese specialities, including a decent choice of soups and seafood. Excellent standards of service can also be expected. Open Mon–Sat noon–2.30pm, 6–10.30pm, Sun from 10.30am.

El Maiz Venezuelan Cuisine $$ *6 Jalan Punchak, off Jalan P Ramlee; tel: 03-2022 1733.* As one of the more popular options for South American cuisine, El Maiz is testament to the growing trend of global foods in the city. The arepas are excellent and the sugar cane with lime provides a refreshing antidote to the heat after walking around the KL Forest Eco Park. Open Mon–Sat 10am–10pm, Sun 11am–6pm.

Hakka Restaurant $$ *6 Jalan Kia Peng; tel: 03-2143 1908.* An established Chinese restaurant near the Jalan Raja Chulan end of Kia Peng, that is the place to come to for authentic Hakka food. Hakka cuisine is salty, fragrant and fatty and features rich, textured sauces. Signature dishes include beggar's chicken (baked salted chicken) and *mui choy kau yoke* (braised pork belly layered with preserved vegetables). Open daily noon–3pm, 6– 11.30pm.

RGB & The Bean Hive $$ *35 Jalan Damai; tel: 03-2181 1329.* This vegetarian and vegan haven is in the residential area of Jalan Damai. The coffee roastery serves up salad sandwiches, humus wraps, healthy vegetarian dishes and vegan cakes. The ingredients are organic to boot. It is a hip place housed in an inconspicuous white bungalow, with no sign indicating there's a café, so just follow the smell of roasting coffee along Jalan Damai. Open Mon–Wed 8.30am–5.30pm, Thu–Sat 8.30am–11.45pm, Sun 9am–6pm.

Still Waters $$$ *Hotel Maya Kuala Lumpur, 138 Jalan Ampang; tel: 03-2711 8866;* www.hotelmaya.com.my. A stylish, serene ambience, with water features all around, sets the mood for *'sosaku'* or creative Japanese cuisine. The balance of fresh Japanese ingredients and cooking styles from all over the world yields unorthodox and interesting results. A Cantonese menu is also available. Open Mon–Fri noon–3pm, Mon–Sat 7–11pm.

BUKIT BINTANG

Enak $$$ *LG2 Feast Floor, Starhill Gallery, 181 Jalan Bukit Bintang; tel: 03-2782 3807.* Step into an elegant interior with brass antiques and sculptures. Creative takes on traditional Achenese and Malay cuisine, beautifully presented. Calorie-counters should note that there is liberal use of coconut milk and deep-frying, but the food is delicious. Open daily noon–midnight.

Li Yen $$$$ *The Ritz-Carlton, 168 Jalan Imbi; tel: 03-2142 8000;* www.ritz carlton.com. Fine Cantonese fare in a sumptuous setting is on offer at this award-winning restaurant. Be pampered by faultless service and enjoy live classical music every evening as you dine on classics such as Peking duck, suckling piglet and pork ribs. There is also an excellent spread of dim sum at lunchtime. Open Mon–Sat noon–2.30pm, 6.30–10.30pm; Sun from 10.30am.

Passage Thru India $$ *4 Jalan Delima, off Jalan Bukit Bintang; tel: 03-2145 0366;* www.passagethruindia.com. In an old bungalow opposite the Royal Selangor Club, this restaurant scores for atmosphere and a menu that lives up to its name with a range of Indian delights, from Goan seafood to meats from Assam. Try the *dum biryani* (a special preparation of rice and spiced meat) and excellent fish *tikka*. Open daily 11.30am–2.45pm, 6.30–10.45pm.

Sahara Tent $$ *41 & 43 Jalan Sultan Ismail; tel: 03-2144 8310;* www.saha ratent.com. This is one of the oldest Arab eateries in Kuala Lumpur, close to the HSBC bank. Its popular buffets are as varied as ever, the notable dishes including creamy humus and tender lamb. Vegetarian options are good, such as the chef's speciality, which features aubergine (eggplant), and the vine-leaf *waraq-enab*. Open Mon–Sat 11am–3am, Sun 11am–midnight.

Sao Nam $$$ *25 Tengkat Tong Shin; tel: 03-2144 1225;* www.saonam.com. my. This eatery features a contemporary approach to traditional Vietnamese cuisine. Highlights include the unique mangosteen salad, Vietnamese pancake and duck in tamarind. A well-priced wine list complements the superb food. Reservations are a good idea. Open daily 12.30–2.30pm, Sun–Thu 7–10.30pm, after 10.30pm drinks only, Fri–Sat 7pm–12.30am.

Weissbräu $$$ *Level 3, Pavilion, 168 Jalan Bukit Bintang; tel: 03-2142 0288;* www.out2dine.com.my. This German bistro dishes up hearty platters of pork sausages, *schnitzel* and a superb pork knuckle, which you can wash down with a range of German beers. For lighter meals, try the regional favourites of the *flammkuchen* or *spätzle*. Open daily 10am–1.30am.

A-Z TRAVEL TIPS

A SUMMARY OF PRACTICAL INFORMATION

A

ACCOMMODATION

Some of Asia's best hotels in every price range can be found in Kuala Lumpur, with the continued glut of rooms ensuring that quality accommodation is affordable. Luxury hotels are extremely reasonable, and good budget accommodation is also available, usually in pre-war shophouses.

The big luxury hotel chains are all here, most located in the Golden Triangle, with views of the Petronas Twin Towers and/or Kuala Lumpur Tower offered as selling points. Bukit Bintang has a range of accommodation, including some interesting three-star boutique hotels. Serviced apartments are becoming quite popular. The more established backpacker hostels are in the old city centre areas around Petaling Street and Tengkat Tong Shin, increasingly with funky 'flashpacking' options.

Published rates usually include 6 percent GST tax and 10 percent service tax, and most include a buffet breakfast. Actual rates are often lower, and discounts can be negotiated for longer stays. Hotels that target business travellers usually offer discounts at weekends. Internet rates are lower than walk-in or call-in rates.

Hotels are open all year round and a surcharge is usually imposed for peak periods: long weekends, Malaysian and Singaporean school holidays and public holidays, particularly Hari Raya Puasa and Chinese New Year, the Formula One Grand Prix period, and the peak Arab tourist period from July to August, when advance bookings are strongly advised up to six months beforehand.

AIRPORTS

There are two international airports, linked by shuttle buses called Airport Liners running from 6am until midnight (the fare is RM3).
KLIA. Over 50 airlines land at Kuala Lumpur International Airport (KUL; tel: 03-8777 7000; www.klia.com.my), a large and modern airport 50km (30 miles) south of KL.

From KLIA, the fastest way to the city centre is by the high-speed KLIA Ekspres train, also known as the ERL (5am–1am, 15-minute intervals during peak hours, 20-minute intervals during off-peak hours and every 30 minutes after midnight; www.kliaekspres.com; RM55), which takes 28 minutes to reach the KL Sentral Station; from there, taxis, inter-city trains and buses are plentiful. Airport Limo taxis take about 60 minutes to reach the city centre. Buy a coupon at the airport (RM75 budget, RM102 premier; 24 hours, 50 percent surcharge midnight–6am). Airport Coach buses take over an hour to reach KL Sentral, departing from the airport basement (www.airportcoach.com.my; 5.30am–1.30am, 30-minute intervals; RM15); they make drop-offs at major hotels en-route.

For departures, the KLIA Ekspres (tel: 03-2267 8000; 5am–12.40am) departs from KL Sentral (Kuala Lumpur City Air Terminal or KL CAT); passengers with a train ticket may check in at least two hours before departure for Malaysia Airlines, Cathay Pacific Airways, Emirates, Etihad Airways and Royal Brunei. The Airport Coach (tel: 03-8787 3894, 5am–11pm) also departs from KL Sentral and its transit vans do pickups from major hotels to KL Sentral.

For pickups, call Airport Limo (tel: 1-300 88 8989; 24 hours) or hail or call any taxi (surcharge, plus meter).

KLIA2. This terminal (built to replace the old LCCT) serves low-cost airlines (KUL; tel: 03-8778 5500; www.klia.com.my). Located less that 2km from KLIA (5 minutes by train), the airport boasts state-of-the art infrastructure, as well as an impressive skybridge linking the main terminal with the satellite building. This is the first Asian airport to have a skybridge, providing wonderful views of the airside.

From KLIA2, you can take the KLIA Ekspres train to the centre of town (4.55am–0.55am) – the journey takes 33 minutes and the fare is exactly the same as the fare from KLIA. The Aerobus runs from KLIA2 to KL Sentral every 30 minutes from 4.30am until 2.30am (www.aerobus. my; RM10). You can also take the Airport Liner shuttle to KLIA to access the transport options described above.

Avoid touts offering 'cheap' taxi rides at both airports – you usually end up paying a lot more. Also note that the Sultan Abdul Aziz Shah or Subang Airport, which services turboprop domestic flights by Berjaya, Malindo Air and Firefly, is 20km (12 miles) from KL (SZB; tel: 03-7842 2773).

B

BUDGETING FOR YOUR TRIP

On average, allow RM300 a day without accommodation, although travelling off-peak and being particularly frugal could cut that down to RM200–250. Below are some indicative costs, but bear in mind that inflation in KL is about 5 percent per year.

Accommodation starts at RM40 for decent budget accommodation. RM200 will get you a good room in a three- or four-star hotel. Rates for five-star hotels start at RM300.

Food is very affordable: RM30 buys you a decent meal with non-alcoholic drinks; a three-course meal in a mid-range restaurant costs about RM50; street food is as low as RM8 for a meal with drinks. Alcohol is very expensive, with beer costing RM14–20 a pop and much more in most clubs.

Transport is cheap if you use trains and buses within the city, and RM15 per day should suffice. Taxis charge RM3 for the first kilometre (half mile), with a 10-sen increase every 115m/yds. From midnight to 6am there is a surcharge of 50 percent on the metered fare. Surcharges also apply for bookings (RM2), baggage placed in the boot (RM1 per piece) and additional passengers beyond two (RM1 each).

Admission fees are generally reasonable for attractions (RM5–20) and theatre performances (RM40–150).

C

CAR HIRE

Driving within KL is not recommended, as traffic is horrendous and signage confusing. However, driving outside the city on excursions is a pleasure.

The minimum age is 18 and an international driver's licence is required, except for tourists from Australia, Japan, the EU, New Zealand, Singapore and the US, who need a valid national licence. Major car-rental companies have 24-hour counters at the KLIA, as well as branches in other major cities where you can drop off your car. Rental starts from RM150 for the compact Malaysian-made Proton car and should include insurance and unlimited mileage. Chauffeur-driven cars are also available. A credit card is usually required as a deposit. Reputable companies include: **Avis Malaysia**, tel: 1800-88 2847, www.avis.com.my; **Europecar**, tel: 019-279 9818, www.europcar.com.my; **Hertz** tel: 03-2715 8383, www.hertz.com; **Kasina Rent-A-Car**, tel: 04-644 1842, www.kasina.com.my and **Mayflower Car Rental**, tel: 03-6253 1888, www.mayflowercarrental.com.my.

CLIMATE

Details on local weather can be found on the Malaysian Meteorological Department homepage: www.met.gov.my.

	J	F	M	A	M	J	J	A	S	O	N	D
Average temp												
°C	27	27	28	28	28	27	27	27	27	27	27	27
°F	81	81	82	82	82	81	81	81	81	81	81	81
Average rainfall												
mm	192	181	251	292	191	133	136	155	197	258	297	247
in	7.6	7.1	11.5	11.5	7.5	5.2	5.4	6.1	7.8	10.2	11.7	9.2

CLOTHING

Cottons and natural fibres work best in Kuala Lumpur's climate. Shorts and T-shirts are generally acceptable, including in shopping malls, although KL-ites do tend to dress up for a night on the town. If you intend to visit places of worship or travel outside of KL, pack clothing that covers your arms and legs. For footwear, slip-ons are handy, as shoes must be removed before entering temples and homes. If you intend to jungle-trek, pack tougher shoes. Sunglasses and umbrellas or raincoats come in handy.

CRIME AND SAFETY

Purse snatching and petty theft are prevalent, so make sure your belongings are secure. Snatch thieves tend to comprise two men on a motorcycle or leaning out of moving cars. If your bag is snatched, let go of it, because many thieves carry knives, which they will not hesitate to use. When walking along the street, always face oncoming traffic and make sure your bag is on your side that is away from the road. Pickpockets operate in crowded areas and on trains and buses.

When sightseeing, only carry what you need, though you are required to have your passport on you. However, police will only ask to see your ID if you have committed a crime or you are unlucky enough to be in a nightspot that is being raided. Never buy anything from touts, whether bus or train tickets or admission tickets to attractions. Report any crime to the nearest police station (tel: 999 or 112 from a mobile phone).

CUSTOMS

Prohibited goods include drugs, dangerous chemicals, pornography, firearms and ammunition. Drug possession carries a mandatory death sentence. Upon arrival in Malaysia, declare all taxable goods; for details, check the Customs website at www.customs.gov.my. You may have to pay a deposit for temporary importation, refundable on departure – usually 50 percent of the value. Keep your receipt of purchase and obtain an official receipt for any tax or deposit paid. Among duty-free items are cameras, watches, pens, perfume, cosmetics and lighters.

D

DISABLED TRAVELLERS

Basic disabled-friendly facilities, like extra-wide parking bays, wheelchair ramps and toilets, can be found in major hotels, malls, theatres, fast-food chains and some government buildings. The Kuala Lumpur International Airport and the Light Rail Transit (LRT) system in Kuala Lumpur are also disabled-friendly. However, the city does not make life easy for people with disabilities. Streets are uneven and sometimes potholed and difficult to navigate, while ramps are inadequate. Taxis will usually not transport people in wheelchairs or will apply additional charges.

DRIVING

Malaysia operates a left-hand driving system. The speed limit is 50kph (30mph) in towns, 80kph (50mph) outside towns, and 90–110kph (56–68mph) on highways. Slow down when you go through a village and before a school, and keep left unless overtaking. The wearing of seat belts is compulsory.

Petrol is slightly over RM2 a litre, and stations are plentiful, even along the highways. Note that road signs are in Bahasa Malaysia and can be inadequate, so buy a good, recent KL road map or download one on a GPS.

Malaysian drivers can be speed maniacs and rule-breakers, while motorcyclists can shoot out from nowhere or hog the road. Heavy rain can be hazardous.

E

ELECTRICITY

Electrical outlets are rated at 220 volts, 50 cycles and serve three-pin, flat-pronged plugs. American products do not work here, but most supermarkets stock adaptors. Major hotels can supply an adaptor for 110–120-volt, 60 Hz-appliances.

EMBASSIES AND CONSULATES

Australia: 6 Jalan Yap Kwan Seng; tel: 03-2146 5555; www.malaysia.embassy.gov.au.

Canada: 17th Floor Menara Tan and Tan, 207 Jalan Tun Razak; tel: 03-2718 3333; www.canadainternational.gc.ca.
New Zealand: 21st Floor Menara IMC, 8 Jalan Sultan Ismail; tel: 03-2078 2533; www.nzembassy.com. Visas are only issued in Singapore.
UK: 27th floor Menara Binjai, 2 Jalan Binjai; tel: 03-2170 2200; www.gov.uk/government/world/malaysia.
US: 376 Jalan Tun Razak; tel: 03-2168 5000; https://my.usembassy.gov.

EMERGENCIES

Police/Ambulance/Fire Brigade: **999** (**112** from mobile phone).

doctor **doctor**
hospital **hospital**
clinic **klinik**
medicine **ubat**
I feel ill. **Saya berasa sakit.**
I need a doctor. **Saya perlu doctor.**
This is an emergency! **Ini kecemasan!**

G

GETTING THERE

By air. Malaysia's national carrier is Malaysia Airlines (MAS; tel: 03-7843 3000, 1300-883 000 toll-free within Malaysia; www.malaysiaairlines.com), which flies to KL from over 100 domestic and international destinations. There are two local budget airlines: AirAsia (www.airasia.com, check the call centre number for your country on the website), which flies to KL from local and regional destinations, and also Australia; and Firefly (tel: 03-7845 4543; www.fireflyz.com.my), run by MAS, which has a turboprop fleet covering Peninsular Malaysia, Singapore, Sumatra (Indonesia) and southern Thailand.

Thai Airways offers international flights via Bangkok and Singapore Airlines via Singapore. From the UK, airlines include Cathay Pacific, Emirates, Etihad, KLM, Lufthansa, Qatar, Singapore Airlines and SriLankan Airlines. Travel time is 13 hours non-stop from Heathrow. From Australia, airlines include Cathay Pacific, China Airlines, Singapore Airlines and Jetstar Airways. Travel time is eight hours from Sydney.

By rail. If you are in Bangkok or Singapore, you can take the train to the KL Sentral Station (Stesen Sentral KL). The KTM (National Railways; tel: 03-2267 1200; www.ktmb.com.my) trains are modern, air-conditioned and efficient. Express services do not stop along the way except for the service from Bangkok, which requires a change of trains in Butterworth. Travel time is 20 hours from Bangkok and eight hours from Singapore.

By road. There are comfortable, air-conditioned express bus services from Bangkok and Singapore to KL. The main bus terminus in town is Pudu Sentral near Petaling Street. Buses from Bangkok terminate at Butterworth, where you change to a local bus, which then takes the excellent North–South Expressway to KL. Travel time is 21 hours. From Singapore, buses take six hours to reach KL.

By sea. KL's closest seaport is Port Klang (Pelabuhan Klang), about 40km (25 miles) southwest, where ferries service the Indonesian towns of Tanjung Balai, Sumatra and Dumai, Riau; this is also the main port of call for cruise ships.

GUIDES AND TOURS

Hotels can generally arrange tours to any of the attractions listed in this book. To avoid scams, make sure tour agencies are registered with the Malaysian Association of Tour and Travel Agents (www.matta.org.my). Prices are usually around RM100 for half-day city tours and RM200–250 for full-day tours. Individual tour guides (Kuala Lumpur Tourist Guides Association, http://kltga.my) and car-and-driver outfits charge by the hour. For insurance purposes, make sure your service agents are licensed.

A great way to get to the main attractions is the **Kuala Lumpur Hop-on Hop-off Bus** (tel: 03-9282 2713; www.myhoponhopoff.com), which makes over 20 stops around the city.

Recommended tour and travel agencies include: Asian Overland Services (tel: 03-4252 9100; www.asianoverland.com.my), Holiday Tours and Travel (tel: 03-6286 6000; www.holidaytours.com.my), Mayflower (tel: 03-9232 1888; www.mayflower.com.my) and Shajasa Travel & Tours (tel: 03-2026 8668; http://shajasa.com.my). Central Market and Be Tourist conduct free heritage walks in the area (tel: 03-2032 1031; www.malaysiaheritage.net), while Simply Enak specialises in food tours (tel: 017-2878 929; www.simplyenak.com).

For nature and adventure tours, contact Asian Overland Services or Endemicguides.com (tel: 016-383 2222; www.endemicguides.com). For white-water sports in Kuala Kubu Bahru, contact the Malaysian Rafting Community (tel: 019-6458 615; www.raftmalaysia.com). For caving tours of the Dark Caves, Batu Caves, book with Cave Management Group (tel: 03-6186 7011; www.darkcavemalaysia.com).

H

HEALTH AND MEDICAL CARE

Malaysia has high health standards, comparable to the US and Western Europe. However, prior to visiting the country, check the Malaysian Ministry of Health website (www.myhealth.gov.my), make sure you buy medical insurance, and get cholera, hepatitis A and B and tetanus shots. Before you travel, check with your doctor whether any other health precautions are necessary. There are periodic outbreaks of dengue fever, for which there is no immunisation, so take preventive measures like using insect repellent, and if you suffer from a very high fever while or shortly after visiting Malaysia, consult a doctor immediately. Those with respiratory disorders should avoid visiting KL during the haze period.

While adjusting to the heat and humidity, hydrate yourself with at least 2 litres (8–10 glasses) of water a day and keep out of the sun between 11am and 1pm. Drink boiled or bottled water or canned drinks. Avoid ice cubes in street-side stalls and small coffee shops, as the ice cubes here are usually made using unboiled water. Refrain from eating cut fruit from stalls.

KL has some of the best doctors in the region, who speak good English. Consultancy starts at RM30 for a GP and RM60 for a specialist. Private clinics *(klinik)* abound, some open 24 hours a day, and pharmacies are also plentiful. Major hotels have on-premises medical services. Government hospitals are well equipped and have specialised clinics, including **Hospital KL** (Jalan Pahang; tel: 03-2615 5555). Private hospitals include **Tung Shin Hospital** (Jalan Pudu, near Pudu Sentral; tel: 03-2037 2288) and **Gleneagles Intan Medical Centre** (Jalan Ampang; tel: 03-4141 3000). Dental work is generally very good quality and reasonably priced. Dental clinics can be found in major shopping malls.

L

LANGUAGE

The official language of Malaysia is Bahasa Malaysia, or Malay. It is also known as Bahasa Melayu and popularly abbreviated to BM. It is an easy language to learn and is written in the Roman alphabet. The language is polysyllabic, with variations in syllables to convey changes in meaning. Words are pronounced as they are spelt. Most Malaysians speak English, albeit in varieties that can be colourful and localised.

1 **satu**
2 **dua**
3 **tiga**
4 **empat**
5 **lima**
6 **enam**
7 **tujuh**
8 **lapan**

9 **sembilan**
10 **sepuluh**
11 **sebelas**
12 **dua belas**
20 **dua puluh**
21 **dua puluh satu**
100 **seratus**
1,000 **seribu**
How do you do? **Apa khabar?**
fine/good **baik**
good morning **selamat pagi**
good afternoon **selamat petang**
good night **selamat malam**
goodbye **selamat tinggal**
bon voyage **selamat jalan**
thank you **terima kasih**
you're welcome **sama-sama**
please **tolong/sila**
excuse me **maafkan saya (maaf)**
May I ask you a question? **Tumpang tanya?**
Where is the toilet? **Tandas di mana?**
I am sorry **minta maaf (maaf)**
What is your name? **Siapa nama anda?**
My name is... **Nama saya...**
yes **ya**
no **tidak (tak)**

LGBTQ TRAVELLERS

KL has perhaps Southeast Asia's most exciting gay scene, according to leading gay portal Utopia-Asia (www.utopia-asia.com/tipsmala.htm). KL-ites are generally tolerant – though not of public displays of affection – and appreciative of the pink dollar, so gay and lesbian visitors can travel safely and without fear of persecution in KL other than very occasional, minor harassment from police. However, there are provisions in the Penal Code and, for Muslims, Islamic Shariah laws, that penalise same-sex sexual acts and cross-dressing. For more information on the gay community, contact the PT Foundation (tel: 03-4044 4611; www.ptfmalaysia.org).

M

MEDIA

The main English-language dailies are *The Star*, *The New Straits Times*, *The Sun* and the tabloid *Malay Mail*. However, these publications tend to be pro-government; more balanced news is provided by online newspaper *Malaysian Insider* and critical political news by *Malaysiakini* (www.malaysiakini.com). Business coverage is provided daily by *The Edge*.

You can also buy *The Wall Street Journal*, *The International Herald Tribune* and *USA Today* at bookshops and hotel newsstands. Local lifestyle and entertainment magazines with news and listings include *Klue*, *Time Out*, *Vision KL* and *Juice*.

Cable TV is available in most hotels, and usually includes CNN, BBC, CNBC and HBO.

MONEY

Currency. Freely convertible, the Malaysian Ringgit (RM), also known as the dollar by the locals, is divided into 100 sen. Bank notes are denominated in units of 1, 2, 5, 10, 50 and 100. Coins are 5, 10, 20 and 50 sen.

Currency exchange. Banks and moneychangers are at many locations, including the main bus and train terminals and the airports. Banks charge a commission whereas moneychangers do not, but the latter's rates differ, so shop around for the best and try bargaining – larger amounts of currency get you better rates.

Credit cards. Visa and MasterCard are most widely accepted; American Express and Diners Club less so. Retailers add an extra 3 percent surcharge for the privilege of using plastic. As with everywhere in the world, be conscious of credit card fraud.

ATMs. ATMs are found in almost all bank branches, and particularly ones in the shopping malls. The operating hours for local machines are 6am–midnight, but some international banks operate 24 hours. Banking networks available are MEPS, Cirrus, Maestro and BANKCARD.

O

OPENING TIMES

Government offices are on a five-day week and follow an 8am to 5pm day. From Mon–Thu, most close for a one-hour lunch break beginning at 12.30 or 1pm. On Fri, the break is from 12.45–2.45pm to allow Muslims prayer time. Some businesses and government departments operate on Sat from 9am–1pm.

Banking hours are 9.30am–4pm Mon–Fri, although banks in shopping malls and areas like Masjid India, KLCC and Mid-Valley open from 10am–7pm weekdays and 10am–1pm on Sat. Moneychangers are open until 7pm daily. Shops open Mon–Sat between 9am and 11am and close between 9 and 11pm; some operate for a few hours on Sun. Shopping mall hours are generally 10am–10pm. There are 24-hour convenience stores all over the city.

Restaurants usually open from 11am–2.30pm and 5–11pm, while café hours are 7am–10pm. Eateries tend to close later at weekends, especially in tourist areas. *Mamak* outlets that serve Indian-Muslim fare are open 24 hours a day, and some hawker centres are open for dinner and only close at 4am.

P

POST OFFICES

Although you take a bit of a chance with regular mail sent via the Malaysian postal service (www.pos.com.my), its registered mail, parcel and courier services (*Poslaju*) are good. You can also cash postal and money orders here. Post offices are found everywhere, and most are open Mon–Fri 8am–5.30pm. The General Post Office (tel: 03-2727 9100; Mon–Fri 8.30am–8pm, Sat 8.30am–5pm) is at Kompleks Dayabumi, beside Central Market. Post offices with extended hours from Mon–Sat are in the Mid-Valley Megamall (9pm), Suria KLCC (6pm, including on Sun) and Sungai Wang Plaza (8pm). There is also a post office in KLIA (main building). Most big hotels can mail a letter for you.

International courier companies include **FedEx** (The Weld Shopping Centre, Jalan Raja Chulan; tel: 1-800 88 6363) and **DHL** (Central Market; tel: 017-8710 805).

PUBLIC HOLIDAYS

Dates of cultural festivals vary as they are determined by lunar calendars. Check precise dates with Tourism Malaysia (see page 128).

1 January New Year's Day
1 February Federal Territory Day
January/February Chinese New Year
1 May Labour Day
May Wesak Day
First Sat in June Agong's Birthday
31 August National Day
16 September Malaysia Day
October/November Deepavali
25 December Christmas
date varies Prophet Muhammad's Birthday
date varies Hari Raya Puasa
date varies Hari Raya Haji

R

RELIGION

When visiting a place of worship, always remove footwear and hats; in mosques, make sure your arms and legs are covered. In Sikh temples, make sure your hair is covered. Be sensitive to the fact that pork is not served or eaten in Muslim-run eateries, beef in Indian Hindu-run eateries, and meat in some Buddhist temples; likewise that Muslims strictly observe the fasting month of Ramadan.

Brickfields is home to churches of virtually all Christian denominations. The main Anglican church is the historic St Mary's Cathedral on Jalan Raja; the main Catholic church, the Cathedral of St John at 5 Jalan Bukit Nanas; and the main Methodist church is Wesley Methodist Church on 2 Jalan Wesley (near Pudu Sentral).

T

TELEPHONES

The country code for Malaysia is 60 and the area code for KL and Selangor is 03, and Pahang, 09. To call KL from overseas, dial the international access code (00 from the UK, 011 from the US or Canada), followed by 603, followed by the number. For local and international telephone-directory assistance and operator-assisted calls, dial 100. To call overseas from KL, dial 00 followed by the country code, area code (omitting the first zero for UK area codes) and phone number.

Most hotels offer International Direct Dial (IDD) services, but charges are high. Alternatively, some prepaid cards offer cheaper rates for international calls to certain destinations.

There are public phones but phone-booth vandalism is high, so it is worth bringing your mobile phone with you if you use the GSM band, as prepaid SIM cards are very affordable, starting at RM20 for registration and air time.

TIME ZONES

The standard Malaysian time is 8 hours ahead of GMT, 7 hours ahead of London (BST), 12 hours ahead of New York (in summer), 6 hours ahead of Johannesburg, 4 hours behind Auckland and 3 hours behind Sydney. The country shares the same time zone with Singapore and Hong Kong.

TIPPING

Tipping is not obligatory, as bills usually include a 6 percent service charge. However, tips are appreciated. Porters are usually tipped RM2–5, restaurant and bar staff are used to being left loose change or the rounding of the bill to the nearest denomination of 5 or 10, but obviously, you may tip according to how you feel about the quality of service. Otherwise, a simple thank you (*terima kasih*) and a smile will do.

TOILETS

KL has a long way to go towards clean public toilets, although some of the ones in shopping malls have improved. Otherwise, expect dirty and wet toilets, and squat ones. Toilet paper is rare, although you can usually buy tissue paper at the toilet entrance. Most malls charge a toilet entrance fee of 30–50 sen. If you are very particular, pop into the nearest hotel and use their toilets.

TOURIST INFORMATION

Tourism Malaysia has a 24-hour infoline, 1300-88-5050 (within Malaysia only) and an excellent website, www.tourism.gov.my. Tourist offices have helpful and trained staff, and ample information in the shape of brochures and maps.

Arrivals at the KLIA can visit the 24-hour **Visitor Service Centre** at the International Arrival Hall, Level 3, Main Building (tel: 03-8776 5651). The main information centre is at the **Malaysia Tourism Centre (MATIC)** at 109 Jalan Ampang (tel: 03-9235 4800; www.matic. gov.my; daily 8am–10pm), which has officers, tourist literature and computers to surf state tourism homepages, a tour agency, the Transnasional interstate coach company, and a restaurant. Cultural performances are held Mon–Sat, while theatre performances are staged sporadically in an auditorium. Tourist information is also available at **KL Sentral**, 2/F, Arrivals Hall, Kuala Lumpur City Air Terminal (tel: 03-2272 5823; daily 9am–6pm).

For a full list of Tourism Malaysia offices overseas, visit www.tourism.gov.my.

KL-specific information is also provided by the Visit KL information centre at the **KL City Gallery** (27 Jalan Raja, Dataran Merdeka; tel: 03-2698 3333; daily 9am–6.30pm) and two other counters in Jalan Bukit Bintang and Jalan P Ramlee. There is also an information centre at Central Market (tel: 1-300 228 688; daily 10am–10pm). Related tourism organisations include **KL Tourist Guides' Association** (tel: 03-9221 0688; http://kltga.my) and **Malaysian Association of Tour and Travel Agents** (tel: 03-9222 1155; www.matta.org.my).

TRANSPORT

Kuala Lumpur's public transport system is modern and efficient. Try to use the trains as much as possible to avoid vehicular traffic, which can be nightmarish during peak hours (7.30–9.30am, 5–7pm) and when it rains. Be sure to carry enough small change for fares, especially when taking taxis.

Trains. Three train systems operate in KL (with a fourth being constructed) and, with a bit of walking, these should get you to all the city's attractions. The Light Rail Transport (**LRT**; tel: 03-7885 2585; www.myrapid.com.my; Mon–Sat 6am–midnight, Sun 6am–11.30pm) has two lines that intersect at Masjid Jamek and serves the Golden Triangle, the old city centre, Kampung Baru and Petaling Jaya. The elevated **Monorail** (daily 6am–11.30pm), also run by RapidKL, covers Petaling Street, Bukit Bintang, Kampung Baru, Brickfields and Titiwangsa. The **KTM Komuter** (tel: 1-300 885 862; www.ktmb.com.my; daily 5am–11.50pm) electrified commuter rail service has two lines that link downtown KL with the Klang Valley conurbation.

The central hub for all rail services is the ultra-modern KL Sentral Station (Stesen Sentral KL; tel: 03-2279 8899; www.stesensentral.com). Consider purchasing stored-value tickets for convenience.

Buses. Several companies provide bus services in KL, but the service is generally poor. RapidKL (tel: 03-7885 2585; www.myrapid.com.my; daily 6am–11pm) has the newest buses, and their City Buses (RM1 per zone) cover downtown KL and link to many LRT stations. The main inner-city bus stops are Central Market/KL Sentral, Bukit Bintang, KLCC and Titiwangsa/Chow Kit. Buses are packed during peak periods, so watch your wallets.

Taxis. Taxis are plentiful in KL, but drivers have a bad reputation for not using meters, which they are legally required to use, refusing to go to certain places and overcharging tourists. The notorious ones hang out at large hotels and major tourist sights. Just walk a little away and flag down a passing taxi. Check before you get into a taxi that they will use the meter and again that they do switch it on after you get in. Find out from your hotel concierge how much a ride should cost, and if you are prepared to pay a flat rate, make sure it is reasonable.

Taxis come in different colours, representing different companies, but all have a *Teksi* sign on their roof, which when lit signals availability. There are also premium taxis that have a RM4 flagfall and charge more per kilometre. Taxis can be hailed at taxi stands or flagged down in the street. KL Sentral and KL Tower have a coupon system, which is more expensive but could end up cheaper than bargaining with a recalcitrant driver. You can also telephone reliable taxi companies such as Comfort (tel: 03-8024 0507), Public Cab (tel: 03-6259 2020), Supercab (tel: 03-7875 7333) and Sunlight (tel: 1-300 800 222). Half- and full-day taxi charters to the Klang Valley cost RM25–30 per hour, excluding toll charges.

I would like to go to... **Saya nak pergi ke...**
How much is the fare? **Berapa harganya?**
Can I get small change? **Boleh tukar duit kecil tak?**
Please use the meter. **Sila guna meter.**

V

VISAS AND ENTRY REQUIREMENTS

Passports must be valid for at least six months at the time of entry. Check the Immigration Department website (www.imi.gov.my) for details about formalities and visa requirements as conditions may change from time to time.

Generally, citizens of the UK, US, Canada, Australia, New Zealand, Ireland, South Africa, most European countries and several other countries do not require a visa for a stay of up to three months. Extensions may be applied for at the immigration office in Putrajaya (tel: 03-8892 6000) or Shah Alam, Selangor (tel: 03-5519 0653).

W

WEBSITES AND INTERNET CAFÉS

Features and information on Kuala Lumpur and Malaysia can be found on travel portal *Journeymalaysia* (www.journeymalaysia.com). For what's happening where in KL, *Time Out Kuala Lumpur* (www.time-outkl.com) provides the most comprehensive information. Gourmands should check out *Fried Chillies* (www.friedchillies.com), which has food reviews galore. Nature-lovers should visit *Wildasia* (www.wildasia.org), which promotes responsible tourism and lists operators and activities.

Internet cafés can be found in major shopping areas like Petaling Street and the KL City Centre, and rates start from RM2 per hour. However, a lot of internet cafés are for gaming and therefore filled with noisy youngsters. If you have your own computer or smartphone, most cafés offer free Wi-Fi (often, the cashier will provide you with the login name and password), but it is still not always free in hotel rooms, especially in some budget accommodation.

RECOMMENDED HOTELS

Tourists have a good choice of international brands, home-grown chains, business hotels, themed resorts and boutique establishments, as well as serviced apartments, simple Chinese-run rest houses and backpacker hostels. Packages may include breakfast and sometimes tours and entrance fees to attractions. If you stay more than one night, you can try bargaining for better rates. Hotels are required to display rates that include all taxes.

Below is a basic guide to the published rates for standard double rooms. Actual rates are usually lower, and internet rates are among the best.

$$$$	over RM400
$$$	RM300–400
$$	RM100–300
$	under RM100

AROUND DATARAN MERDEKA

BackHome Kuala Lumpur $ *30 Jalan Tun H.S. Lee; tel: 03-2022 0788; www.backhome.com.my.* This thoughtfully renovated backpacker hostel spreads across a row of shophouses within walking distance to the Pudu Sentral bus terminus and Petaling Street. Beds are comfy and have partitions for privacy. All rooms have washbasins and there is also a female-only dorm. A nice touch is an open-air chilling-out section.

Reggae Mansion Kuala Lumpur $ *53 Jalan Tun H.S. Lee; tel: 03-2072 6877; www.reggaehostelsmalaysia.com/mansion.* A beautifully converted colonial building, this trendy budget hostel has all the backpacker facilities, as well as private sleeping cubicles, an open courtyard and a fantastic rooftop bar, which is naturally always busy. Double rooms are also available if dorm rooms are not your preference. Only online bookings accepted.

PETALING STREET

Ancasa Hotel & Spa $$ *Jalan Tun Tan Cheng Lock; tel: 03-2026 6060;* www.ancasahotels.com. This hotel has a great location in a bustling area within walking distance of the Pudu Sentral bus terminus and right next to Petaling Street. In addition, there is a free shuttle service to the KLCC, Masjid Jamek, KL Sentral and Bukit Bintang. The rooms are comfortable and some have great views of the skyline.

Hotel China Town 2 $ *70–72, Jalan Petaling; tel: 03-2072 9933;* www.ho telchinatown2.com. Here you'll find simple and clean accommodation that is halfway between a hotel and a hostel. Rooms can be a little noisy, being in the thick of Petaling Street, but the location is very convenient. All rooms have air-conditioning and en-suite bathrooms with hot show-ers, but only some have windows. Facilities include internet access, lockers, laundry and telephones.

Matahari Lodge $ *58-1, Jalan Hang Kasturi; tel: 03-2070 5570;* www. matahari-lodge.kualalumpurshotels.com. This well-regarded accom-modation has clean and comfortable rooms and dorms, and is close to transport links and sights. Loads of travel and tourism information is available. However, bring earplugs, particularly for rooms on the third floor, which hosts the common areas.

JALAN MASJID INDIA AND KAMPUNG BARU

Coliseum Café and Hotel $ *98–100 Jalan Tuanku Abdul Rahman; tel: 03-2692 6270.* Immerse yourself in the old-world charm of these rooms that date back to the 1920s. One of the first hotels in town, it housed less sa-lubrious colonial characters who would drown their sorrows in the bar downstairs. Today, backpackers fill the 10 rooms and the view includes laundry drying on lines above the rooftops.

Tune Hotel – Downtown Kuala Lumpur $ *316 Jalan Tuanku Abdul Rah-man; tel: 03-7962 5888;* www.tunehotels.com. This hotel uses the same formula as budget airlines (it is in fact linked to AirAsia): book online in advance or take advantage of special offers to get really low rates, although refunds are not allowed. The simply decorated, almost-bare rooms have specially designed beds that assure guests of a good night's sleep, and the showers are luxurious.

LAKE GARDENS AND BRICKFIELDS

Carcosa Seri Negara $$$$ *Persiaran Mahameru, Taman Botani Perdana (Lake Gardens); tel: 03-2295 0888;* www.temptingplaces.com. This hotel offers a luxurious stay in a beautifully restored colonial mansion with manicured gardens. In keeping with its past, the Carcosa continues to host dignitaries from around the world. Each suite is different, some coming with a terrace and others with separate dining, dressing and living rooms.

Cititel Mid Valley $$ *Mid Valley City, Lingkaran Syed Putra; tel: 03-2296 1111;* www.cititelmidvalley.com. This business hotel is right by Mid Valley City's two enormous malls, so it is great for shopaholics, especially since the hotel is directly connected to one of the malls. The standard rooms are small but clean and have nice views. There is easy access to trains.

Hilton Kuala Lumpur $$$$ *3 Jalan Stesen Sentral; tel: 03-2264 2264;* www.hilton.com. Soak up the style of this hip and happening Hilton with its luxurious beds, rainforest showers and huge plasma TVs. The rooms are bright, and floor-to-ceiling windows give great views of the city. There is also a fancy multi-restaurant and bar enclave, and the main KL Sentral train terminus is opposite the hotel.

PODs the Backpackers Home $ *1-6, No 30 Jalan Thambipillay, Brickfields; tel: 03-2276 0858;* http://podsbackpacker.com. A fun outfit in one of the oldest ungentrified parts of town, this hostel offers great free extras like step-bike tours, performance evenings and meditation sessions. Rooms are basic but the atmosphere is great. It is within walking distance of KL Sentral, which also makes it a great place to shower and rest before a journey.

KLCC

Concorde Hotel $$$ *2 Jalan Sultan Ismail; tel: 03-2144 2200;* http://kualalumpur.concordehotelsresorts.com. This is a central, busy hotel close to nightlife and trendy eateries. It has a popular lounge, which attracts weekend crowds spilling over from the adjoining Hard Rock Café. The better rooms are in the Premier wing, which overlooks the Bukit Nanas forest reserve.

Fraser Place $$$$ *Lot 163 No 10, Jalan Perak; tel: 03-2118 6288;* http://kualalumpur.frasershospitality.com. Computers for free use, an excellent coffee machine and fruit in the lobby set the tone for the amenities that these serviced apartments offer guests. All bedrooms come with living, dining and study areas, as well as a fully equipped kitchen, and the excellent housekeeping ensures everything is tip-top.

GTower Hotel $$$ *199 Jalan Tun Razak; tel: 03-2168 1919;* www.gtowerhotel.com. Ultra-modern and stylish, this business hotel is purportedly the first in Malaysia to be constructed using green principles. From its central location, great city skyline views can be had from its upper-floor pool, bars and restaurants, including a funky space on a bridge across its two towers.

Hotel Maya $$$ *138 Jalan Ampang; tel: 03-2711 8866;* www.hotelmaya.com.my. Award-winning interior design and personalised service are hallmarks of this contemporary hotel. Highlights of the rooms in this boutique resort hotel include rustic timber flooring and floor-to-ceiling glass panels overlooking either the Twin Towers or Kuala Lumpur Tower; the guests-only Sky Lounge provides views of both.

Impiana KLCC Hotel $$$ *13 Jalan Pinang; tel: 03-2147 1111;* http://kualalumpurhotels.impiana.com.my. This chic hotel is perfect for business travellers, as it is located very close to the Kuala Lumpur Convention Centre and other important business areas of the city. The rooms are elegant with free Wi-Fi and comfortable bedding; some offer sweeping views of the KL panorama. The luxurious hotel spa will keep you relaxed.

Mandarin Oriental Kuala Lumpur $$$$ *Kuala Lumpur City Centre; tel: 03-2380 8888;* www.mandarinoriental.com/kualalumpur. In a prime position next to the Petronas Twin Towers, this super-luxury hotel boasts attentive service and large, well-appointed rooms. Club rooms command fabulous views of the Twin Towers. There is a wide choice of good restaurants, with breakfasts often described as the best buffets in town.

Pacific Regency Hotel Suites $$$ *KH Tower, Jalan Punchak, off Jalan P. Ramlee; tel: 03-2332 7777; www.pacific-regency.com.* Located a little away from the madding crowd, this five-star serviced apartment hotel perches opposite the KL Tower. Choose from studios and two-bedroom, family-style units, all with fully equipped kitchenettes and free Wi-Fi access. There is an in-house mini-mart and delicatessen. The chic rooftop Luna Bar has great 360-degree views of the skyline.

Shangri-La Hotel Kuala Lumpur $$$$ *11 Jalan Sultan Ismail; tel: 03-2032 2388; www.shangri-la.com/kualalumpur.* Just across the road from the pulsating clubs of Jalan P. Ramlee and close to the KL Tower, this large hotel has comfortable, capacious rooms and lovely gardens. Popular among business folk, its foyer is always busy and the lounge often crowded. Likewise, its restaurants are good but popular at weekends, so bookings are essential.

Traders Hotel $$$$ *Kuala Lumpur City Centre; tel: 03-2332 9888; www.shangri-la.com/traders.* Connected to the Kuala Lumpur Convention Centre, this is a chic, contemporary hotel that caters to a mainly business clientele, but offers the same efficient treatment to tourists, too. It's worth paying extra for the park-view rooms, which offer stunning views of the KLCC Park and the Petronas Twin Towers. Come sundown, be sure to head up to the wonderful SkyBar for a cocktail.

BUKIT BINTANG

Bintang Warisan Hotel $$ *68 Jalan Bukit Bintang; tel: 03-2148 8111; www.bintangwarisan.com.* In the heart of Bukit Bintang, this place has surprisingly good facilities once the rather cluttered lobby is negotiated. The location is superb and double-glazed windows keep out the noise; nonetheless, it is best to get a room on a higher floor. There are rooms for three and four people, too.

Dorms KL $ *5 Tengkat Tong Shin, Bukit Bintang; tel: 03-2110 1221.* Located along the backpackers' row, this 24-hour hostel scores points for its warm family atmosphere. Some great backpacker facilities are available, including copious tourist information, a relaxing common area and an on-site café lounge selling local dishes. Dorms and private rooms are available.

Hotel Capitol Kuala Lumpur $$$ *Jalan Bulan, off Jalan Bukit Bintang; tel: 03-2143 7000; www.capitolhotel-kualalumpur.com.* While its lower-floor rooms can be noisy, this hotel's luxurious new '10 rooms' suites on the 19th and 20th floors are quiet and spacious, with 4m (13ft) high ceilings as standard and the largest suite measuring 56 sq m (602 sq ft). The modern decor includes comfortable sofas and lovely prints of KL, as well as floor-to-ceiling windows.

JW Marriott Kuala Lumpur $$$$ *183 Jalan Bukit Bintang; tel: 03-2715 9000; www.marriott.com.* Designed for the business traveller, this hotel has all the requisite mod cons, including separate work areas in the rooms. The hotel is part of the Starhill Gallery complex, so guests can use the mall's spa and health facilities, as well as charging dining expenses at the 13 upscale restaurants in the basement Feast Village to their rooms. The hotel lobby can be very busy because it is linked to the mall, but Bukit Bintang and all that it offers is right on your doorstep.

Rainforest Bed & Breakfast $$ *27 Jalan Mesui, off Jalan Nagasari; tel: 03-2145 3525; https://rainforestbedandbreakfast.blogspot.com.* This pretty hostel makes good its name with a lush, green setting and wood and bamboo indoors. Located off the Changkat Bukit Bintang party strip, it has comfortable beds, clean bathrooms and a designated balcony for smokers. The staff are knowledgeable and there is easy access to public transport, sights and eateries for every budget.

The Ritz-Carlton Kuala Lumpur $$$$ *168 Jalan Imbi; tel: 03-2142 8000; www.ritzcarlton.com/en/hotels/malaysia/kuala-lumpur.* Linked to Starhill Gallery, this luxury boutique hotel's personalised butler service is its trademark. With an area of 45 sq m (484 sq ft) and ceilings 3m (9ft) high, the guest rooms are also among KL's largest. Indulge in outdoor spa baths and a wide range of therapies at its beautiful tropical Spa Village.

Sarang Vacation Homes $$ *4 Jalan Sin Chew Kee; tel: 012-333 5666, 012-210 0218 (mobile);* www.sarangvacationhomes.com. Experience a Malaysian home-from-home in these houses, which date back to the 1920s. Available for rent as rooms or in their entirety, the houses are homey, comfortable and friendly. This interesting concept has racked up a good reputation and rates include great local breakfasts and Wi-Fi. A minimum two-day stay is required during peak periods.

The Westin Kuala Lumpur $$$$ *199 Jalan Bukit Bintang; tel: 03-2731 8333;* www.thewestinkualalumpur.com. Located at one end of the busy Jalan Bukit Bintang next to Starhill Gallery and opposite The Pavilion shopping mall, this contemporary hotel boasts superbly comfortable beds, a good Kids' Club and babysitting services, as well as the popular Latin venue, Qba. The gym is excellent and there is even a guided scenic morning run through the KLCC Park.

OUTSIDE KUALA LUMPUR

Hilton Petaling Jaya $$$ *2 Jalan Barat, Petaling Jaya; tel: 03-7955 9122;* www.hilton.com. Primarily a business hotel, this Hilton is conveniently located in Petaling Jaya New Yotn close to public transport links to KL and lots of shops and eateries. Don't miss the outstanding Malaysian spread at its popular restaurant, Paya Serai.

Kuala Selangor Nature Park $ *Jalan Klinik; tel: 03-3289 2294;* www.kuala-selangor.com. Staying at the park is the best way to hear dawn bird choruses and gorgeous moonlit sonatas, as well as catch sight of otters and monkeys. Accommodation is in basic chalets and a dormitory, and you need to bring your own towels and toiletries, but there is cold running water and 24-hour electricity. Come well prepared for mosquitoes. For meals, walk 10 minutes to the old town centre.

Puncak Inn, Fraser's Hill $$ *Tel: 09-362 2007;* www.puncakinn.pkbf.gov. my. Located in the centre of Fraser's Hill and incorporating the tourist information centre and a gift shop, this hotel's simple rooms are a great value option. Be sure to book early in peak seasons though as this spot is frequently fully booked.

Resorts World Genting $$$$ *tel: 03-2718 1118 (Kuala Lumpur)*; www. rwgenting.com. Choose from the five-star Maxims Genting Hotel and Highlands Hotel or the three-star Theme Park Hotel (where the indoor theme park sits) and First World Hotel (one of the world's largest hotels). Rooms at the lower star-rated hotels are small and peak-period check-ins excruciatingly slow. The Awana Hotel, tel: 03-6436 9000, midway up, is less hectic and is set in lovely green surroundings.

Sunway Resort Hotel and Spa $$$$ *Persiaran Lagoon; tel: 03-7492 8000*; www.sunwayhotels.com/sunwayresorthotelspa. A Malaysian version of South Africa's Palace of the Lost City, this is a hit with families as it is just a short walk away from the Sunway Lagoon theme park and Pyramid shopping centre. It has a great landscaped swimming pool and an excellent Italian restaurant. Part of the hotel is underground; avoid rooms just beneath the lobby, as it can be noisy overhead.

Ye Olde Smokehouse Hotel and Restaurant, Fraser's Hill $$$ *Jalan Jeriau; tel: 09-362 2226*; www.thesmokehouse.my. This former Red Cross building boasts beautiful stone masonry, well-manicured English gardens and sumptuous Devonshire cream teas. While slightly worn, rooms are cosy and offer a choice of hill or garden views. Common areas are filled with chintz and memorabilia. A fire is lit every evening, and guests are required to dress for dinner.

DICTIONARY

ENGLISH-MALAY

adj adjective **adv** adverb **BE** British English **n** noun **prep** preposition **v** verb

A

a.m. pagi
accept v menerima
access masuk
accident kemalangan
accommodation penginapan
account n akaun
adapter adaptor
address n alamat
admission (fees) bayaran masuk
after selepas
afternoon tengah hari
aftershave losen selepas bercukur
again semula; lagi
age umur
agency agensi
AIDS AIDS
air udara
air conditioning alat hawa dingin; penyaman udara
airline sistem penerbangan
airmail mel udara
airplane kapal terbang
airport lapanpan terbang
airport tax cukai penerbangan
aisle seat tempat duduk tepi lorong
aisle lorong; ruang sayap

alarm clock jam loceng
alcohol alkohol; arak
allergic reaction reaksi alah
allergic alah; alergi
allow v membenarkan
alone sendirian
alter v (clothing) meminda (pakaian)
alternate route jalan yang lain
aluminum foil kerajang aluminium
amazing mengagumkan
ambulance ambulans
American orang Amerika
amount jumlah; amaun
amusement park taman hiburan
anemic penyakit anemia
anesthesia n ubat bius
animal haiwan
ankle buku lali; pergelangan kaki
antibiotic antibiotik
antiques store kedai antik
antiseptic cream krim antiseptik
anyone sesiapa
anything apa-apa

apartment pangsapuri; apartmen
appendix (body part) umbai usus
appetizer pembuka selera
apple epal
appointment janji temu
apricot aprikot
arcade arked
area code kod kawasan
arm tangan
around (the corner) di sebalik (selekoh)
arrivals (airport) ketibaan
arrive v tiba
artery arteri
arthritis artritis
artificial sweetener pemanis tiruan
Asian (restaurant) restoran Asia
asparagus pucuk asparagus
aspirin aspirin
assistance pertolongan; bantuan
asthma penyakit lelah; asma
ATM card kad ATM
attached (in a relationship) sedang menjalin hubungan

attack (on person) serangan
attend v menghadiri
attraction (place) tempat menarik
attractive menarik
audio audio
Australian warga Australia
authentic asli
automatic car kereta automatik

B

baby bottle botol bayi
baby food makanan bayi
baby wipe tisu lembap untuk bayi
baby bayi
babysitter pengasuh bayi
back (body part) belakang
backpack beg galas
bacon bakon
bag beg
baggage BE bagasi
baggage claim tuntutan bagasi
baggage ticket tiket bagasi
bake v membakar
bakery kedai roti
ballet balet (tarian)
banana pisang

bandage pembalut

bank bank

bar (place) bar

barbecue barbeku

barber tukang gunting rambut

baseball besbol

basket (grocery store) bakul

basketball bola keranjang

bathroom bilik air

batik kain batik

battery bateri

battleground tempat pertempuran

be v menjadi

beach pantai

bean curd tauhu

beautiful cantik

bed and breakfast tempat penginapan dengan sarapan pagi

bed katil

beef daging lembu

beer bir

before sebelum

begin v bermula

beginner (skill level) orang yang baru belajar

behind (direction) belakang

beige kuning air

belt tali pinggang

berth tempat berlabuh

best terbaik

bet v bertaruh

better lebih baik

beverage minuman

bicycle basikal

big besar

bigger lebih besar

bike route jalan basikal

bikini bikini

bill v **(charge)** bil; ~ n **(money)** wang kertas

bird burung

birthday hari jadi

bites n gigitan

black pepper lada hitam

black hitam

bladder pundi kencing

bland tawar

blanket selimut

bleed v berdarah

blood pressure tekanan darah

blood darah

blouse blaus; baju wanita

blow-dry (hair) ditiup kering

blue biru

board v menaiki

boarding pass pas masuk

boat bot; sampan

boil (cooking method) rebus

bone tulang

book n buku; v menempah

bookstore kedai buku

boots kasut but

boring bosan

botanical garden taman botani

bother v ganggu, menggangu

bottle opener pembuka botol

bottle botol

bowl mangkuk

box kotak

boxing match pertandingan tinju

boy budak lelaki

boyfriend teman lelaki

bra coli

bracelet rantai tangan; gelang tangan

brakes (car) brek

brave adj berani

bread roti

breaded (cooking method) bersalut serbuk roti

break v pecah

break down v rosak

breakfast sarapan pagi

break-in (burglary) kejadian pecah rumah; rompakan

breast buah dada

breastfeed menyusu bayi dengan susu ibu

breathe deeply tarik nafas

breathe v bernafas

bridge jambatan

briefs (clothing) seluar dalam

bring v membawa

British orang British

broccoli brokoli

broken (bone) patah; **(machine)** rosak; **(glass)** pecah

brooch kerongsang

broom penyapu

brother (older) abang

brother (younger) adik

brown coklat; perang

bug pepijat

building bangunan

burn v membakar

bus station stesen bas

bus stop perhentian bas

bus ticket tiket bas

bus tour persiaran dengan bas

bus bas

business bisnes; perniagaan

business center pusat perniagaan

business class kelas perniagaan

business hours waktu perniagaan

busy sibuk

butcher penjual daging

butter mentega

buttocks punggung

buy v membeli

bye selamat jalan

C

cabbage kubis

cabin kabin

cable car kereta kabel

café kafe

call v panggil; ~ n panggilan telefon

calories kalori

camera case sarung kamera

camera store kedai kamera

camera kamera

camp v berkhemah

camping stove dapur khemah

campsite tapak perkhemahan

can opener pembuka tin

can n tin; ~ **(yes)** boleh

Canadian warga Kanada

cancel v membatalkan

candy gula-gula

canned goods makanan tin

canyon kanyon

capsicum lada benggala

car hire *[BE]* menyewa kereta

car park *[BE]* tempat meletak kereta

car rental sewa kereta

car seat tempat duduk kereta

car kereta

carafe serahi

carambola (starfruit) belimbing

card kad

carp (fish) ikan kap

carrot lobak merah

carry-on beg tangan

cart troli

carton karton

carvings, *n* ukiran

cash *n* wang tunai; ~ *v* tunaikan cek

cash advance wang pendahuluan

cashier juruwang

casino kasino

castle istana kota

cathedral gereja besar

Catholic Katolik

cauliflower kubis bunga

cave gua

CD CD

celery saderi

cell phone telefon mudah alih; telefon bimbit

Celsius Celsius

centimeter sentimeter

ceramic spoon sudu seramik

cereal bijian

certificate sijil

chair lift (cable car) lif kerusi

chair kerusi

change *v* menukar; tukar; ~ *n (money)* wang kecil

charcoal arang

charge *v (credit card)* membayar

cheap murah

cheaper lebih murah

check *v (something)* memeriksa (sesuatu); ~ *n* cek

check-in mendaftar masuk

check-out mendaftar keluar

checking account akaun semasa

cheese keju

chemical toilet tandas kimia

chemist *[BE]* ahli kimia

cheque *[BE]* cek

cherry ceri

chest (body part) dada

chest pain sakit dada

chewing gum gula-gula getah

chicken ayam

child kanak-kanak; budak

child's seat kerusi budak

children's portion bahagian kanak-kanak

China negara Cina

china tembikar

Chinese (person) orang Cina

chocolates coklat

chopsticks penyepit

church gereja

cigar cerut

cigarette rokok

city hall dewan bandar raya

clam kepah

class kelas

classical music muzik klasik

clay pot belanga

clean *v* membersihkan; ~ *adj* bersih

cleaning product produk membersih

cleaning supplies bahan membersih

clear *v* batal

cliff cenuram

clock jam

close *v* tutup; ~ *adj* dekat

closed tertutup

clothing store kedai pakaian

clothing pakaian; baju

club kelab

coat kot

cod (type of fish) ikan kod

coffee shop kedai kopi

coin duit syiling

cola kola

cold dingin; sejuk

cold (sickness) selsema

colleague rakan sekerja

collect call panggilan pindah bayaran

cologne air kolong

color warna

comb sikat

come *v* datang

company (firm) syarikat

complain mengadu

complaint aduan

computer komputer

concert hall dewan konsert

concert konsert

condition (medical) keadaan (kesihatan)

conditioner (hair) perapi (rambut); kondisioner

condom kondom

conference persidangan

confirm *v* mengesahkan

congestion kesesakan

connect *v (internet)* menyambung

connection (internet) sambungan

constipated sembelit

consulate pejabat konsul; konsulat

consultant pakar runding

contact *v* berhubungan

contact lens kanta sentuh

contact lens solution cecair pencuci kanta sentuh

contagious berjangkit

contain mengandungi

convention hall dewan persidangan

conversion table jadual pertukaran

conveyor belt tali sawat penyampai

cook *v* memasak

cooking gas gas memasak

cool (temperature) dingin; agak sejuk

copper kuprum

corkscrew skru pencungkil gabus

corn (vegetable) jagung

corner selekoh

cost harga; kos

costume jewelry barang kemas kostum; hiasan

cot katil budak

cotton kapas

cough batuk

counter n kaunter

country code kod negara

court (sports) gelanggang

cover charge bayaran masuk

crab (animal) ketam

cramps (menstruation) kejang datang haid

crash v (car) kemalangan

cream/ointment krim; krim salap

credit card kad kredit

crew neck kolar berbentuk bulat

crib katil bayi

crystal krystal

cup cawan

cured meat daging awet

currency exchange office pejabat pertukaran wang asing

currency exchange pertukaran wang asing

currency mata wang

current account [BE] akaun semasa

customs kastam

cut v (hair) menggunting; ~ n (injury) luka

cute comel

cycling mengayuh basikalcigar

D

dairy hasil tenusu

damage v merosakkan, n kerosakan

damaged telah rosak

dance club kelab menari

dance v menari

dancing sedang menari

danger bahaya

dark gelap

date (calendar) tarikh

dates (fruit) kurma

day hari

deaf pekak

debit card kad debit

decision keputusan

deck chair kerusi dek

declare v mengisytiharkan; mendeklarasi

decline v (credit card) menolak

deeply jauh ke dalam

degrees (temperature) darjah

delay v menangguh; n penangguhan; kelewatan

delete v memadam

delicatessen delikatesen

delicious sedap

denim kain demin

dentist doktor gigi

denture gigi palsu

deodorant penyahbau

department store kedai serbaneka

departure perlepasan

deposit v memasukkan; ~ n (bank) menabung

detergent bahan cuci

diabetes penyakit kencing manis

dial v mendail

diamond berlian

diaper kain lampin

diarrhea cirit-birit

diesel minyak diesel

difficult susah

digital photo gambar digital

digital print cetakan gambar digital

dining room ruang makan

dinner makan malam

direction arah

dirty kotor

disabled accessible [BE] mesra kurang upaya

disabled kurang upaya; cacat

disconnect (computer) memberhentikan sambungan

discount diskaun

dish (kitchen) pinggan mangkuk

dishes (food) lauk-pauk

dishwasher mesin basuh pinggan mangkuk

dishwashing liquid cecair pencuci pinggan mangkuk

display case kotak pameran

display v mempamerkan; n pameran

disposable razor pencukur pakai buang

disposable pakai buang

dive v menyelam

diving equipment kelengkapan menyelam

divorce v bercerai; n perceraian

dizzy pening

do not disturb janggan ganggu; janggang kacau

doctor doktor

dog anjing

doll patung

dollar (U.S.) dolar

domestic flight penerbangan domestik

domestic domestik

door pintu

dormitory asrama

double bed katil kelamin

downtown pusat bandar

dozen dozen

draw lukis; melukis

drawer laci

dress (piece of clothing) baju

dress code kod pakaian

drink menu menu minuman

drink v minum; ~ n minuman
drinking water air minuman
drive v memandu
driver's license number nombor lesen memandu
drop (medicine) titik
drowsiness kepeningan
dry cleaner kedai mencuci kering
duck (animal) itik
during semasa
duty (tax) cukai; duti
duty-free bebas cukai
DVD DVD

E

ear telinga
earache sakit telinga
early awal
earrings anting-anting
east timur
easy senang
eat v makan
economy class kelas ekonomi
egg telur
eggplant [aubergine] terung ungu
elbow siku
electric outlet saluran elektrik
elevator tangga gerak
e-mail address alamat e-mel
e-mail e-mel
emergency exit pintu keluar kecemasan
emergency kecemasan
empty kosong; v mengosongkan

end v tamat
engaged (in a relationship) bertunang
English Inggeris
engrave v mengukir
enjoy v menikmati
enter v masuk
entertainment hiburan
entrance pintu masuk
envelope sampul surat
epilepsy epilepsi
equipment kelengkapan; perkakasan
escalator tangga gerak; eskalator
e-ticket tiket elektronik
evening petang
excess lebihan
exchange rate kadar pertukaran wang asing
exchange v menukar
excursion rombongan
excuse me v maafkan saya
excuse n alasan
exhausted amat letih; keletihan
exit v keluar; ~ n pintu keluar
expensive mahal
expert (skill level) pakar
expiration date tarikh lupus
express ekspres
extension (phone) sambungan
external use
extra large (size) (saiz) tambah

extra small (size) (saiz) lebih kecil
extra tambahan
extract v (tooth) mencabut
eye mata

F

fabric kain
face muka
facial rawatan muka
facility kemudahan
family keluarga
fan (appliance) kipas
far jauh
fare (e.g taxi fare) tambang
farm ladang; kebun
far-sighted (eye condition) rabun dekat
fast food makanan segera
fast cepat
faster lebih cepat
fat free bebas lemak
father ayah; bapa
fax number nombor faks
fax v menghantar faks; ~ n faks
fee bayaran
feed v menyuap
ferry feri
fever deman
field (sports) padang
fill out v (form) mengisi
fill up v (food) menambah
filling (tooth) tampalan
film (camera) filem
fine (fee) denda
fine (greetings) khabar baik

finger jari
fingernail kuku jari
fire api
fire department jabatan api dan bomba
fire door pintu penghadang api
first pertama
first class kelas pertama
fit (clothing) muat
fitting room bilik mencuba pakaian
fix v (repair) membaiki
fixed-price menu menu dengan harga tetap
flashlight lampu suluh
flats (shoes) kasut tidak bertumit
flight penerbangan
floor lantai
florist penjual bunga
flower bunga
fly v terbang; menerbang
fly (insect) lalat
folk music muzik rakyat
food makanan
foot kaki
football game [BE] perlawanan bola sepak
for untuk
forecast ramalan
forest hutan
fork garpu
form (fill-in) borang
formula (baby) susu bayi
fountain pancuran air
free bebas

freezer penyejuk beku
fresh segar
fried (cooking method) goreng
friend kawan; rakan
fruits buah-buahan
frying pan kuali leper
full penuh
full-service perkhidmatan penuh
fun berseronok
funny lucu

G

game permainan
garage garaj
garbage bag beg sampah
garlic bawang putih
gas station stesen minyak
gas minyak
gate (airport) pintu
gay (happy) meriah; riang
gel (hair) gel
get off (a train/bus/subway) turun
get to pergi ke
gift hadiah
gin gin
girl gadis; anak perempuan
girlfriend teman wanita
give v memberi
glass (drinking) gelas
glass (material) kaca
glasses (spectacles) cermin mata
gluten gluten
go v **(somewhere)** pergi
gold emas
golf course padang golf

golf tournament pertandingan golf
good baik; bagus
good afternoon selamat tengah hari
good evening selamat petang
good morning selamat pagi
goodbye selamat jalan
goods barangan
grandchild cucu
grandchildren cucu-cicit
grandfather datuk
grandmother nenek
grape anggur
grapefruit limau gedang
grater pemarut
gray kelabu
green hijau
grocery store kedai runcit
ground floor tingkat bawah
group kumpulan
guide (tourist) n pemandu (pelancong)
guide book buku panduan
guide dog anjing pemandu
gym gim
gynecologist doktor pakar puan

H

hair dryer alat pengering rambut
hair salon salum rambut
hair rambut
hairbrush berus rambut

haircut potongan rambut
hairspray penyembur rambut
hairstyle gaya rambut
hairstylist pendandan rambut
halal halal
half hour setengah jam
half setengah
half-kilo setengah kilo
hall dewan
ham (food) ham
hammer tukul
hand luggage [BE] bagasi tangan
hand tangan
handbag [BE] beg tangan
handicapped kurang upaya; cacat
handicapped-accessible mesra kurang upaya
hangover pening kerana terlalu
happy gembira
hat topi
have v mendapatkan
hawker centre pusat makanan
hay fever deman alergi
head (body part) kepala
headache sakit kepala
headphones fonkepala
health food store kedai makanan sihat
health kesihatan
hearing impaired cacat pendengaran
heart condition sakit jantung
heart jantung

heat haba
heater pemanas
heating [BE] memanas
height ketinggian
hello helo
helmet topi keledar
help pertolongan; bantuan
here sini I
hi hai
high tinggi
highchair kerusi tinggi budak
high-heels kasut bertumit tinggi
highlights (hair) penyerlah
highway lebuhraya
hill bukit
hire v [BE] menyewa
hired car [BE] kereta sewa
hitchhike v mengembara tumpang
hockey hoki
hold v pegang
holiday [BE] percutian
home rumah
hospital hospital
hostel asrama
hot (temperature) panas; ~ **(spicy)** pedas
hot water air panas
hotel rumah; rumah penginapan
hour jam
house rumah
household goods barangan rumah
housekeeping services perkhidmatan mengemas bilik
how are you apa khabar

how much (price) berapa

how bagaimana

hug v memeluk

hungry lapar

hurt sakit

husband suami

I aku, saya

ibuprofen ibuprofen (see painkiller)

ice ais

icy berais; sangut sejuk

identification (card) (kad) pengenalan

ill sakit

immigration imigrasi

in dalam

include v termasuk

indoor dalam rumah

indoor pool kolam renang dalaman

inexpensive murah

infected terjangkit

infection jangkitan

information maklumat

information desk kaunter keterangan

insect bite gigitan serangga

insect repellent penghalau serangga

insert v (on an ATM) memasukkan

inside dalam

insomnia insomnia

instant message mesej segera

insulin insulin

insurance insurans

insurance company syarikat insurans

interested minat; tertarik

interesting menarik

international antarabangsa

international flight penerbangan antarabangsa

international student card kad pelajar antarabangsa

internet cafe kafe internet

internet service perkhidmatan internet

internet internet

interpreter penterjemahan

intersection persimpangan

into ke dalam

introduce v memperkenalkan

invoice invois

Irish orang Ireland

iron (clothes) v menyeterika; ~ n besi

itemize butiran

J

jacket jaket

jackfruit buah nangka

jade jed

jam (food) jem

jam (traffic) n kesesakan; v sesak

jar balang

jaw rahang

jazz club kelab muzik jaz

jazz muzik jaz

jeans seluar jean

jelly (food) agar-agar

jeweler kedai emas

jewelry barang kemas

join v menyertai

joint (body part) sendi

joke bergurau; bersenda

juice jus

K

keep simpan

keep refrigerated simpan sejuk

key kunci; ~ card kad kunci

key ring cecincin kunci

kick tendang

kiddie pool kolam renang budak

kidney (body part) buah pinggang

kilogram kilogram

kilometer kilometer

kind (person) baik hati

kiss v mencium

kitchen dapur

kiwi fruit buah kiwi

knee lutut

knife pisau

know tahu

knowledge pengetahuan

L

lactose intolerant penyakit kurang upaya memproses laktosa

lady wanita; perempuan

lake tasik

lamb (meat) kambing

lamp lampu

language bahasa

large besar

last terakhir

last night malam tadi; semalam

last week minggu yang lalu

late (time) lewat

later nanti

laundromat kedai dobi layan diri

laundry kain kotor

laundry facility kemudahan tempat mendobi

laundry service perkhidmatan mendobi

lawyer peguam

lazy malas

leaded (fuel) (minyak) berplumbum

leaf daun

learn, v belajar

leather kulit

leave (depart) v berlepas (planes); bertolak (buses, trains, etc.)

left (direction) kiri

leg kaki

lemon lemon

lemonade air lemon

lemongrass serai

lens kanta

less kurang

lesson (learnt a lesson) pengajaran

letter surat

lettuce selada

library perpustakaan

licence lesen

life boat bot keselamatan

life jacket jaket keselamatan

lifeguard anggota penyelamat

lift lif

light *n* lampu; ~ *v* **(cigarette)** menyalakan

light *adj* **(bright)** terang; *adj* **(not heavy)** ringan

lightbulb mentol

lighter pemetik api

like *v* suka

lime limau nipis

line garis; barisan

lip bibir

liquor store kedai arak

liter liter

little sedikit

live *v* tinggal

liver (body part) hati

loafers kasut lepak

lobster udang galah

local tempatan

lock *n* mangga

lock up mengunci

locker gerobok; lokar

log off log keluar

log on log masuk

long sleeves lengan panjang

long panjang

long-sighted *[BE]* rabun dekat

look *v* melihat; tengok

lose *v* **(something)** hilang

lost and found hilang dan terjumpa

lost sesat

lotion losen

loud bising

love cinta

low rendah

luggage bagasi

luggage cart troli bagasi

luggage locker lokar bagasi

lunch makan tengah hari

lung paru-paru

M

magazine majalah

Madam/Mrs Puan

magnificent menakjubkan

mail *v* menghantar surat; ~ *n* surat

mailbox peti surat

main attraction tempat tarikan utama

main course hidangan utama

make up (face) *v* bersolek

Malay Melayu

mall pasar raya

man lelaki

manager pengurus

mango buah mangga

manicure rias tangan dan kuku

manual car kereta manual

map *n* peta

market pasar

married telah berkahwin

marry *v* mengahwini

mass (church service) Misa

massage pengurutan

mat (rug) tikar

match *n* mancis

meal hidangan

measure *v* **(someone)** mengukur

measuring cup cawan ukuran

measuring spoon sudu ukuran

mechanic mekanik

medicine ubat

medium (size) sederhana

meet *v* **(someone)** bertemu

meeting room bilik mesyuarat

meeting mesyuarat

membership card kad keahlian

memorial (place) tugu peringatan

memory card kad memori

mend *v* membaiki

men's lelaki

menstrual cramp sakit perut akibat haid

menstruation datang bulan; haid

menu menu

message pesanan

meter (parking) meter

microwave ketuhar gelombang mikro

midday *[BE]* tengah hari

midnight tengah malam

mileage perbatuan

milk susu

mini-bar bar mini

minute minit

Miss Cik

missing (something) hilang; **(someone)** rindu

mistake kesilapan

mobile phone *[BE]* telefon mudah alih; telefon bimbit

mobility pergerakan

money duit; wang

monorail monorel

month bulan

mop mop

more lebih

morning pagi

mosque masjid

mother ibu; emak

motion sickness mabuk gerakan

motor boat motorbot

motorcycle motorsikal

motorway (highway) *[BE]* lebuhraya

mountain gunung

mousse (hair) mousse

mouth mulut

movie theater panggung wayang

movie wayang

Mr/Sir Encik

Mrs/Madam Puan

mug *v* merompak

multiple-trip (ticket) (tiket) pelbagai perjalanan

muscle otot

museum muzium

mushroom cendawan

music store kedai muzik

music muzik

N

nail kuku

name nama

napkin napkin

nappy *[BE]* kain lampin

nationality kewarganegaraan

nature preserve kawasan hutan simpan

nauseous rasa mual

near dekat; nearby berdekatan
near-sighted berpandangan dekat
neck leher; ~lace rantai leher
need v memerlukan
new baru
newspaper surat khabar
newsstand gerai surat khabar
next to sebelah
next seterusnya
nice baik
night malam
nightclub kelab malam
no tidak; bukan
non-alcoholic tanpa alkohol
non-smoking dilarang merokok
noodles mee
noon tengah hari
north utara
nose hidung
notes [BE] nota
nothing tiada apa-apa
notify v menghubungi
novice (skill level) baru belajar
now sekarang
number nombor
nurse jururawat
nuts (food) kacang

O

office pejabat
oatmeal bubur oat
octopus sotong kurita
office hours waktu pejabat
oil minyak
OK OK

old (person) tua; **(long ago)** lama
old town bandar lama
olive buah zaitun
on the corner di selekoh
once sekali
one satu
one-way (ticket) sehala
one-way street jalan sehala
only hanya
on-time tepat masa
open buka
opera opera
opposite bertentangan
optician pakar optik
orange (color) oren
orchestra orkestra
order v memesan
outdoor pool kolam renang luar
outside di luar
over the counter (medication) dijual di kaunter
overdone melampau
overnight bermalam
ox lembu jantan
oxtail ekor lembu
oyster tiram

P

p.m. petang
pacifier puting
pack v mengemas
package bungkusan
pad (for menstruation) [BE] tuala wanita
paddling pool [BE] kolam renang kanak-kanak

pages (in a book) muka surat
pain sakit
painkiller ubat tahan sakit
pajamas baju tidur
palace istana
pants seluar panjang
pantyhose sarung kaki wanita
papaya (fruit) betik
paper towel kertas tisu
paper kertas
paracetamol [BE] panadol **(see painkiller)**
park v meletak kereta; ~ n taman
parking lot tempat meletak kereta
parking meter meter meletak kereta
part-time sambilan
passenger penumpang
passport control kastam dan imigresen
passport pasport
password kata laluan
pastry shop kedai pastri
path lorong; laluan kecil
pay phone telefon awam
pay v membayar
pea kacang pis
peach pic
peak (of a mountain) puncak
pear pir
pearl mutiara
pedestrian pejalan kaki
pediatrician doktor pakar kanak-kanak

pedicure rawatan kaki
peeled (cooking method) tanpa kulit
pen pen
penicillin penisilin
penis zakar
pepper lada
per se-; ~**hour** sejam; ~**day** sehari; ~**night** semalam; ~**week** seminggu
perfume minyak wangi
period (menstrual) datang bulan; haid
period (of time) jangka masa
permit v membenarkan
personal identification number (PIN) nombor pengenalan diri
petite kecil molek
petrol [BE] petrol
petrol station [BE] stesen petrol
pewter piuter
pharmacy farmasi
phone v menelefon; ~ n telefon
phone call panggilan telefon
phone card kad telefon
phone number nombor telefon
photo gambar
photocopy fotokopi
photography fotografi
pick up (something) mengutip
picnic area kawasan berkelah
piece keping
pill (birth control) pil pencegah hamil

pillow bantal
pineapple nanas
pink merah jambu
pizzeria kedai pizza
place n tempat
plan rancangan; pelan
plane kapal terbang
plastic plastik
plastic wrap
pembalut plastik
plate pinggan
platform pelantar
platinum platinum
play v bermain; ~ n
(theatre) sandiwara
playground taman
permainan
playpen kandang main
please sila
pleased gembira
plum buah plum
plunger pelocok
plus size saiz tambah
poach (cooking
method) reneh
pocket poket
poison racun
police polis
police report laporan
polis
police station balai
polis
pomegranate buah
delima
pomelo limau bali
pond kolam
pool kolam renang
pop music muzik pop
porcelain porselin
pork daging babi
porridge bubur
portion bahagian
post [BE] pos
post office pejabat
pos

postbox [BE] peti surat
postcard poskad
pot periuk
potato kentang
pottery (goods)
tembikar
poultry ayam
pregnant hamil
prescribe v mem-
preskripsikan
prescription
preskripsi
press v (clothing)
menyeterika
price harga
print v mencetak
problem masalah
prohibit v melarang
pronounce v menyebut
Protestant Protestan
public awam
pull v menarik
purple ungu
purpose tujuan
purse dompet wanita
push v menolak
pushchair [BE] kerusi
sorong bayi

Q

quality kualiti
queen ratu
question soalan
queue barisan
quick cepat
quiet sunyi; senyap

R

rabbit arnab
radio radio
radish lobak putih
railway station [BE]
stesen kereta api
rain n hujan
raincoat baju hujan

rainforest hutan hujan
ramp tanjakan
rap (music) muzik rap
rape rogol
rare (object) jarang
rash n ruam
rate (exchange rate)
kadar
rat tikus
ravine gaung
raw mentah
reach v tiba
read baca; membaca
ready sedia
real benar; tulen
really sangat; sungguh
reason alasan; sebab
receipt resit
receive v menerima
recharge v mengecas
semula
recommend v
mencadangkan;
mengesyorkan
recommendation
cadangan
recycling kitar semula
red merah
refrigerator peti sejuk
refund bayaran balik
region rantau
registered mail surat
berdaftar
regular (normal)
biasa
relationship
hubungan
rent v menyewa
rental car kereta sewa
repair v memperbaiki
repeat v mengulangi
reservation desk
kaunter tempahan
reservation tempahan
reserve v menempah

resort (holiday)
tempat peranginan
restaurant restoran
restroom (formal/
informal) bilik air/
tandas
retired bersara
return (something)
v mengembalikan;
~ (return ticket) n
[BE] ulang-alik
reverse v (the
charges) [BE] (caj)
balikan
rib (body part) tulang
rusuk
rice nasi
right (direction) kanan
right of way hak
lalu-lalang
ring cincin
river sungai
road jalan
road map peta jalan
roast v memanggang
rob v merompak
robbed dirompak
romantic romantis
room bilik
room (double) bilik
kelamin
room (single) bilik
bujang
room key kunci bilik
room service servis
bilik
round-trip ulang-alik
rotten busuk
rubbish [BE] sampah
rubbish bag [BE] beg
sampah
ruins puing
run lari; melari
rush (in a rush)
kesuntukan masa

S

signature tandatangan
sad sedih
safe (object) peti keselamatan; **~ (protected)** selamat
sales tax cukai jualan
salmon ikan salmon
salon salun
salty masin
sandals kasut sandal
sanitary napkin tuala wanita
sauce sos
saucepan periuk
sauna mandi sauna
sausage sosej
sauteed (cooking method) masak secara saute
save v simpan
savings (account) akaun simpanan
scallion (spring onion) daun bawang
scanner pengimbas
schedule n jadual waktu (perjalanan)
school sekolah
science sains
scissors gunting
sea laut
seafood makanan laut
seat tempat duduk
seaweed rumpai laut
security keselamatan
see v melihat
self-service layan diri
sell v menjual
send v menghantar
senior citizen orang tua
separated (marriage) berpisah

service (in a restaurant) perkhidmatan
sexually transmitted disease penyakit kelamin
shampoo syampu
sharp tajam
shaving cream krim cukur
sheet kain cadar
shellfish kerang-kerangan
ship v (mail) menghantar dengan kapal
shirt kemeja
shoe store kedai kasut
shoes kasut
shop kedai
shopping v membelibelah
shopping area kawasan membeli-belah
shopping centre [BE] pusat membeli-belah
shopping mall pasar raya
short sleeves lengan pendek
short adj pendek
shorts seluar pendek
short-sighted [BE] rabun jauh
shoulder bahu
show v menunjukkan
shower (to wash) mandi hujan
shrimp udang
sick sakit
side dish hidangan sampingan
side effect kesan sampingan

sightseeing tour lawatan
sightseeing melawat tempat-tempat
silk sutera
silver perak
single (unmarried) bujang
single bed katil bujang
single room bilik bujang
sink sink
Sir/Mr Encik
sister (elder) kakak; **(younger)** adik
sit v duduk
size saiz
skin kulit
skirt skirt
sleep v tidur
sleeping bag beg tidur
slice (of something) hirisan
slippers selipar
slower lebih perlahan
slowly perlahan-lahan
small kecil
smaller lebih kecil
smoke v merokok
smoking area kawasan merokok
snack bar bar snek
snacks snek
sneaker kasut sukan
snorkeling equipment kelengkapan snorkel
snow n salji
soap sabun
soccer bola sepak
sock sarung kaki
soda air soda
some sedikit
soother [BE] puting untuk bayi

sore throat sakit kerongkong
sorry minta maaf
soup sup
sour masam
south selatan
souvenir store kedai cenderahati
souvenir cenderahati
soy bean kacang soya
soymilk susu soya
spa spa
spare ribs tulang rusuk
sparkling water air bergas
speak v bercakap
special istimewa; khusus
specialist (doctor) (doktor) pakar
specimen spesimen
speeding memandu melebihi had laju
spell v mengeja
spicy pedas
spinach bayam
spine (body part) tulang belakang
spoon sudu
sporting goods barangan sukan
sports massage pengurutan sukan
sports sukan
sprain terseliuh (v)
squid sotong
stadium stadium
stairs tangga
stamp v (a ticket) mengecap; **~** n **(postage)** stem
start v bermula
starter [BE] pembuka selera

station stesen

statue tugu

stay v menginap

steak stik

steal v mencuri

steam n wap air

steamed (cooking method) dikukus

steamer pengukus

steep curam

sterling silver perak tulen

sting n sengat

stolen telah dicuri

stomach perut

stomachache sakit perut

stop v berhenti

store directory papan panduan kedai

storey [BE] tingkat

stove dapur

straight ahead terus ke hadapan

straight lurus

strange pelik

strawberry strawberi

stream (school) jurusan

stream anak sungai

stroller kereta sorong bayi

student pelajar

study v belajar

stunning menakjubkan

style (hair) gaya

subtitle sari kata

subway station stesen kereta api bawah tanah

subway kereta api bawah tanah

sugar gula

suit sut

suitcase beg pakaian

sun matahari

sunblock losen pelindung matahari

sunburn selaran matahari

sunglasses cermin mata hitam

sunny cerah

sunstroke strok matahari

supermarket pasar raya

supervision penyeliaan; pengawasan

surfboard papan luncur air

swallow v menelan

sweater baju panas

sweet (taste) manis

sweets [BE] gula-gula

swelling bengkak

swim v berenang; ~ **suit** baju renang

swordfish ikan todak

symbol (keyboard) simbol

syrup sirap

T

table meja

tablet (medicine) pil (ubat)

take (something) v mengambil

take away (food) [BE] bungkus (makanan)

take off v **(clothes)** tanggal

tampon tampon

taste v rasa

taxi teksi

tea teh

team pasukan

teaspoon sudu the

telephone telefon

temperature suhu

temple (religious) kuil; tokong

temporary sementara

tennis tenis

tent khemah; ~ **peg** pasak khemah; ~ **pole** tiang khemah

terminal (airport)

terminal (lapangan terbang)

terrible teruk

text v **(send a message)** menghantar teks

thank v berterima kasih

thank you terima kasih

that itu

theater panggung wayang; teater

theft kecurian

there sana

thief pencuri

thigh paha

thirsty dahaga

this ini

thrash [rubbish] sampah

throat kerongkong

thunderstorm ribut petir

ticket tiket; ~ **office** pejabat tiket

tie (clothing) tali leher

tight adj ketat

tights [BE] seluar sama sendat

time masa; ~**table** [BE] jadual waktu

tire tayar

tired letih

tissue tisu

to go pergi ke

toasted bread roti bakar

tobacconist penjual barang-barang tembakau

today hari ini

toe jari kaki; ~**nail** kuku kaki

toilet [BE] tandas

toilet paper tisu tandas

tomorrow esok

tongue lidah

tonight malam ini

too juga

tooth gigi; ~**paste** ubat gigi

top up card (phone value) kad tambah nilai

total (amount) jumlah

tough (food) liat

tour melancong; lawatan

tourist information office pejabat maklumat pelancong

tourist pelancong

tow truck trak penarik

towel tuala

tower menara

town bandar; ~ **hall** dewan bandar

town square pusat pekan

toy mainan

traces sisa-sisa

track (train) landasan

traditional tradisional

traffic light lampu isyarat

trail denai
train keretapi
transfer v (trains/flights) menukar
translate v menterjemah
trash sampah
travel agency agensi perlancong
travel sickness mabuk kembara
traveler's check cek kembara
treat (to a drink) belanja
tree pokok
trim (hair cut) memepat
trip perjalanan
trolley [BE] troli
trousers [BE] seluar panjang
T-shirt baju kemeja-T
turn off (lights) padamkan
turn on (lights) pasangkan
TV televisyen
type v menaip
tyre [BE] tayar

U

ugly hodoh
umbrella payung
unattended tanpa diawasi
unconscious tidak sedarkan diri
underground [BE] bawah tanah
underground station [BE] stensen bawah tanah
underpants [BE] seluar dalam

understand v faham
underwear pakaian dalam
unemployed penganggur
United Kingdom United Kingdom (U.K.)
United States (U.S.) Amerika Syarikat
university universiti
unleaded (gas) minyak tanpa plumbum
unlimited tanpa had
upper bahagian atas
upset stomach sakit perut
urgent penting
urine air kencing
use v menggunakan

V

vacancy kekosongan
vacation percutian
vaccination pemvaksinan
vacuum cleaner permbersih hampagas
vagina faraj
vaginal infection jangkitan faraj
valid sah laku
valley lurah
valuable bernilai
value nilai
vegetable sayur-sayuran
vegetarian tidak makan daging
vehicle kenderaan
vehicle registration pendaftaran kenderaan

vending machine mesin layan diri
very amat
viewpoint [BE] sudut pandangan
village kampung
visa visa
visit v melawat
visiting hours waktu melawat
visually impaired cacat penglihatan
vitamin vitamin
V-neck kolar V
volleyball game permainan bola tampar
vomit v muntah

W

wait v tunggu
waist pinggang
waiter pelayan lelaki
waiting room bilik menunggu
waitress pelayan perempuan
wake v bangun
wake-up call panggilan pagi
walk v berjalan
wall clock jam dinding
wallet dompet
war memorial tugu peringatan
warm v (something) memanaskan; ~ adj (temperature) panas
wash v membasuh; mencuci
washing machine mesin basuh
watch jam tangan
water skis ski air
waterfall air terjun

watermelon tembikai
wear v memakai
weather cuaca
weave v menganyam
week minggu; ~end hujung minggu
weekly setiap minggu
welcome v selamat datang
well-rested rehat secukupnya
west barat
what apa
wheelchair kerusi roda; ~ ramp tanjakan kerusi roda
when bila
where di mana
white putih
who siapa
widowed janda
wife isteri
window tingkap
windsurfer peluncur air
wine list senarai wain
wireless internet service kemudahan internet tanpa wayar
wireless phone telefon tanpa wayar
with dengan
withdraw v mengeluarkan
withdrawal (bank) pengeluaran
without tanpa
woman wanita
wool bulu kambing biri-biri
work (function) berfungsi
work v bekerja; n perkerjaan
wrap v membalut

wrestling perlawanan gusti
wrist pergelangan tangan
write v menulis; n tulisan

Y

year tahun
yellow kuning
yes ya
yesterday semalam

yoghurt yogurt
you anda; kamu
you're welcome sama-sama
young muda
your anda; kamu

youth hostel asrama belia

Z

zoo zoo
zucchini zukini

MALAY–ENGLISH

A

ada to be; to have
abang brother (older)
adaptor adapter
adik younger brother/ sister
aduan complaint
agar-agar jelly (food)
agensi agency
agensi perlancong travel agency
ahli kimia chemist/ pharmacist
AIDS AIDS
air water
air bergas sparkling water
air kencing urine
air kolong cologne
air lemon lemonade
air minuman drinking water
air panas hot water
air terjun
air soda soda
air terjun waterfall
ais ice
akan shall; will
akaun account
akaun semasa check-ing/current account
akaun simpanan savings account

aku I; me
alah allergic
alamat address
alamat e-mel e-mail address
alasan excuse; reason
alat hawa dingin air conditioning
alat pengering rambut hair dryer
amat very
ambulans ambulance
Amerika Syarikat United States (U.S.)
anak child
anak sungai stream
anda you; your
anggota penyelamat lifeguard
anggur grape
anjing dog
anjing pemandu guide dog
antarabangsa international
antibiotik antibiotic
anting-anting earrings
apa what
apa khabar how are you
apa-apa anything
api fire

aprikot apricot
arah direction
arak alcohol
arang charcoal
arked arcade
arnab rabbit
aromaterapi aroma-therapy
arteri artery
artritis arthritis
asli authentic
aspirin aspirin
asrama dormitory
asrama hostel
asrama belia youth hostel
ATM ATM
audio audio
automatik automatic
awal early
awam public
awas danger
ayah father
ayam chicken/poultry

B

baca; membaca read
badminton badminton
bagaimana how
bagasi baggage/ luggage
bagasi tangan hand luggage

bagus good
bahagian portion
bahagian atas upper
bahagian kanak-kanak children's portion
bahan cuci detergent
bahan membersih cleaning supplies
bahasa language
bahaya dangerous
bahu shoulder
baik good; nice
baik hati kind (person)
baju dress; clothing
baju hujan raincoat
baju kemeja-T T-shirt
baju panas sweater
baju renang swimsuit
baju tidur pajamas
bakon bacon
bakul basket (for groceries)
balai polis police station
balang jar
balet ballet
balikan reverse
bandar town
bangun wake v
bangunan building
bank bank
bantal pillow

bar bar (place)
bar snek snack bar
barang kemas jewelry
barangan goods
barangan rumah household goods
barat west
barbeku barbecue
barisan line; queue
baru new
baru belajar novice (skill level)
bas bus
basikal bicycle
basikal berenjin moped
batal clear v
bateri battery
batuk cough
bawah tanah subway/ underground
bawang putih garlic
bayam spinach
bayaran fee
bayaran balik refund
bayaran masuk admission/cover charge
bayi baby
bebas free
bebas cukai duty-free
bebas lemak fat free
beg bag
beg galas backpack
beg pakaian suitcase
beg sampah garbage bag
beg tangan carry-on; handbag
beg tidur sleeping bag
bekerja work
belajar learn
belajar study
belakang back (body part); behind (direction)

belanga clay pot
belanja treat (to a drink)
belimbing carambola (starfruit)
benar real
bengkak swelling
berais icy
berani brave
berapa how much (price)
bercakap speak
bercerai divorce
berdarah bleed
berdekatan nearby
berenang swim
berfungsi work (function)
berhenti stop
berhubungan contact
beri to give
beri jalan give way (on the road)
berjalan to walk
berjangkit contagious
berkhemah to camp
berlepas to depart (planes)
berlian diamond
bermain to play
bermalam overnight
bermula to begin
bernafas breathe
bernilai valuable
berpandangan dekat near-sighted
berpisah separated (marriage)
berplumbum leaded (fuel)
bersalut serbuk roti breaded (cooking method)
bersara retired
berseronok fun

bersolek make up (face)
bertaruh bet
bertemu meet (someone)
bertentangan opposite
berterima kasih to thank
bertolak depart (bus/ train)
bertunang engaged (in a relationship)
berus rambut hairbrush
besar big; large
besbol baseball
betik papaya (fruit)
biara monastery
biasa regular (normal)
bibir lip
bijian cereal
bila when
bilik room
bilik air bathroom
bilik bujang single room
bilik kelamin double room
bilik mencuba pakaian fitting room
bilik menunggu waiting room
bilik mesyuarat meeting room
bir beer
biru blue
bising loud
blaus blouse
bola keranjang basketball
bola sepak soccer
boleh to be able; can
bomba fire brigade
borang form (fill-in)

bosan boring
bot keselamatan life boat
bot boat
botol bottle
brek brakes (car)
brokoli broccoli
buah-buahan fruit
buah dada breast
buah delima pomegranate
buah mangga mango
buah nangka jackfruit
buah pinggang kidney (body part)
buah zaitun olive
bubur porridge
budak child
budak lelaki boy
bujang single (unmarried)
buka open
bukan not
bukit hill
buku book
buku panduan guide book
bulan month
bulu kambing biri-biri wool
bunga flower
bungkus take away (food)
bungkusan package
burung bird
busuk rotten
butiran itemize

C

cacat handicap
cacat pendengaran hearing impaired
cadangan recommendation
cantik beautiful

cawan cup
cawan ukuran measuring cup
cecair liquid
cecair pencuci kanta sentuh contact lens solution
cecair pencuci pinggan mangkuk dishwashing liquid
cecincin kunci key ring
cek check/cheque
cek kembara traveler's check
cendawan mushroom
cenderahati souvenir
cenuram cliff
cepat fast
cerah sunny
ceri cherry
cermin mata glasses/spectacles
cermin mata hitam sunglasses
cerut cigar
cetakan gambar digital digital print
Cik Miss
cincin ring
cinta love
cirit-birit diarrhea
coklat chocolates
coli bra
comel cute
cuaca weather
cucu grandchild
cucu-cicit grandchildren
cukai duty (tax)
cukai jualan sales tax
cukai penerbangan airport tax
curam steep

D

dada chest (body part)
daging awet cured meat
daging babi pork
daging lembu beef
dahaga thirsty
dalam in; inside
dalam rumah indoor
dapur kitchen; stove
darah blood
darjah degrees (temperature)
datang come
datuk grandfather
daun leaf
daun bawang scallion (spring onion)
daun kari curry leaves
dekat near
delikatesen delicatessen
deman fever
deman alergi hay fever
denai trail
denda fine (fee)
dengan with
dewan hall
dewan bandar town hall
dewan persidangan convention hall
di luar outside
di mana where
di sebalik around (the corner)
di selekoh on the corner
dia he, it, she
dijual di kaunter over the counter (medication)

dikukus steamed (cooking method)
dilarang merokok no smoking
dingin cool (temperature)
dirompak robbed
diskaun discount
ditiup kering blow-dry (hair)
doktor doctor
doktor gigi dentist
doktor pakar kanak-kanak pediatrician
doktor pakar puan gynecologist
dolar dollar
domestik domestic
dompet wallet
dompet wanita purse
duduk sit
duit syiling coin
duit money

E

ekor tail
ekspres express
emak mother
emas gold
e-mel e-mail
Encik Mr/Sir
epal apple
epilepsi epilepsy
esok tomorrow

F

faham understand
faraj vagina
farmasi pharmacy
feri ferry
filem film (camera)
fonkepala headphones
fotografi photography
fotokopi photocopy

G

gabus cork
gadis girl
gambar photo
ganggu bother; harass
garaj garage
garis line
garpu fork
gas memasak cooking gas
gaung ravine
gaya style (hair)
gelanggang court (sports)
gelap dark
gelas glass (drinking)
gembira happy
gerai surat khabar newsstand
gereja church
gerobok locker
gigi tooth
gigi palsu denture
gigitan bites
gigitan serangga insect bite
gim gym
goreng fried (cooking method)
gua cave
gula sugar
gula-gula candy
gula-gula getah chewing gum
gunting scissors
gunung mountain

H

haba heat
hadiah gift
hai hi
haid menstruation
haiwan animal
hak lalu-lalang right of way

halal permissible according to Islamic law
hamil pregnant
hanya only
harga cost; price
hari day
hari ini today
hari jadi birthday
hasil tenusu dairy
hati liver (body part)
helo hello
hiburan entertainment
hidangan meal
hidangan sampingan side dish
hidangan utama main course
hidung nose
hijau green
hilang lose (something)
hilang dan terjumpa lost and found
hirisan slice (of something)
hitam black
hodoh ugly
hoki hockey
hoki ais ice hockey
hubungan relationship
hujan rain
hujung minggu weekend
hutan forest
hutan hujan rainforest

I

ialah is
ibu mother
ikan fish
ikan todak swordfish
imigrasi immigration
Inggeris English
ini this

insurans insurance
internet wayarles wireless internet
invois invoice
istana palace
istana kota castle
isteri wife
istimewa special
itik duck (animal)
itu that

J

jabatan api dan bomba fire department
jadual pertukaran conversion table
jadual waktu schedule; timetable
jagung corn (vegetable)
jaket jacket
jaket keselamatan life jacket
jalan road
jalan basikal bike route
jalan sehala one-way street
jalan yang lain alternate route
jam clock; hour
jam dinding wall clock
jam loceng alarm clock
jam tangan watch
jambatan bridge
janda widowed
jangan do not
jangka masa period (of time)
jangkitan infection
janji temu appointment
jauh far

jauh ke dalam deeply
jed jade
jem jam (food)
juga too
jumlah total (amount)
jururawat nurse
jurusan stream (school)
juruwang cashier
jus juice
jantan male
jantung heart
jarang rare (object)
jari finger
jari kaki toe

K

kabin cabin
kaca glass (material)
kacang nuts (food)
kacang pis pea
kacang soya soy bean
kad card
kad keahlian membership card
kad kredit credit card
kad kunci key card
kad memori memory card
kad pengenalan identification card
kad perniagaan business card
kad tambah nilai top up card (phone value)
kad telefon phone card
kadar rate (exchange rate)
kafe café
kain fabric
kain cadar sheet
kain kotor laundry
kain lampin diaper

kakak elder sister
kaki foot; leg
kalori calories
kambing lamb (meat)
kamera camera
kampung village
kamu you; your
kanak-kanak child
kanan right (direction)
kandang main playpen
kanta lens
kanta sentuh contact lens
kapal terbang airplane
kapas cotton
karton carton
kasino casino
kastam customs
kastam dan imigresen passport control
kasut shoes
kasut bertumit tinggi high-heels
kasut but boots
kasut lepak loafers
kasut sukan sneaker
kata laluan password
katil bed
katil bayi crib
katil bujang single bed
katil kelamin double bed
Katolik Catholic
kaunter counter
kawan friend
kawasan berkelah picnic area
kawasan hutan simpan nature preserve
kawasan membeli-belah shopping area

kawasan merokok smoking area

ke dalam into

keadaan condition (medical)

kecemasan emergency

kecil small

kecil molek petite

kecurian theft

kedai store

kedai cenderahati souvenir store

kedai dobi layan diri laundromat

kedai mainan toy store

kedai mencuci kering dry cleaner

kedai roti bakery

store kedai runcit grocery

kedai serbaneka department store

kegunaan luar external use

kejang datang haid cramps (menstruation)

keju cheese

kekosongan vacancy

kelab club

kelab malam nightclub

kelab menari dance club

kelab muzik jaz jazz club

kelabu gray

kelas class

kelas ekonomi economy class

kelas perniagaan business class

kelas pertama first class

kelengkapan equipment

kelengkapan menyelam diving equipment

kelengkapan snorkel snorkeling equipment

keluar exit

keluarga family

kemalangan accident

kemeja shirt

kemudahan facility

kenderaan vehicle

kentang potato

kepah clam

kepala head (body part)

kepeningan drowsiness

keping piece

keputusan decision

kerajang aluminium aluminum foil

keramat Malay shrine

kerang-kerangan shellfish

kereta car

kereta api bawah tanah subway

kereta sewa rental car

kereta sorong bayi stroller

keretapi train

kerongkong throat

kerongsang brooch

kertas paper

kertas tisu paper towel

kerusi chair

kerusi budak child's seat

kerusi roda wheelchair

kerusi tinggi budak highchair

kesan sampingan side effect

keselamatan security

kesesakan congestion

kesihatan health

kesilapan mistake

kesuntukan masa rush (in a rush)

ketam crab (animal)

ketat tight

keterangan information

ketibaan arrivals (airport)

ketinggian height

ketuhar gelombang mikro microwave

kewarganegaraan nationality

khabar baik fine (greetings)

khemah camping; tent

kipas fan (appliance)

kiri left (direction)

kitar semula recycling

kod kawasan area code

kod negara country code

kod pakaian dress code

kola cola

kolam pond

kolam renang swimming pool

kolam renang luar outdoor pool

kolan renang dalaman indoor pool

kolar collar

komputer computer

kondom condom

konsert concert

kopi coffee

kosong empty

kot coat

kota fort

kotak box

kotor dirty

krim cream; ointment

krim cukur shaving cream

krystal crystal

kuali wok

kuali leper frying pan

kualiti quality

kubis cabbage

kubis bunga cauliflower

kuil temple (religious)

kuku nail

kuku jari fingernail

kuku kaki toenail

kulit leather; skin

kumpulan group

kunci key

kunci bilik room key

kuning yellow

kuning air beige

kuprum copper

kurang less

kurang upaya handicapped

kurma date (fruit)

L

laci drawer

lada pepper

lada benggala capsicum

ladang farm

lalat fly (insect)

laluan pejalan kaki walking route

lampu lamp

lampu isyarat traffic light

lampu suluh flashlight

landasan track (train)

lantai floor
lapanpan terbang airport
lapar hungry
laporan polis police report
lari; melari run
lauk-pauk dishes (food)
laut sea
lawatan sightseeing tour
layan diri self-service
lebih more
lebih baik better
lebih besar bigger
lebih cepat faster
lebih kecil smaller
lebih murah cheaper
lebih perlahan slower
lebihan excess
lebuhraya highway
leher neck
lelaki man
lembu ox
lengan panjang long sleeves
lengan pendek short sleeves
lesen licence
letih; keletihan tired; exhausted
lewat late (time)
liat tough (food)
lidah tongue
lif lift
limau bali pomelo
limau gedang grapefruit
limau nipis lime
liter liter
lobak merah carrot
lobak putih radish
lokar locker
lorong alley; path

losen lotion
losen pelindung matahari sunblock
losen selepas bercukur aftershave
lucu funny
lukis; melukis draw
lukisan painting
lurah valley
lurus straight
lutut knee

M

maaf sorry
maafkan saya excuse me
mabuk drunk
mabuk gerakan motion sickness
mabuk kembara travel sickness
mahal expensive
mainan toy
majalah magazine
makan eat
makan malam dinner
makan tengah hari lunch
makanan food
makanan bayi baby food
makanan laut seafood
makanan segara fast food
makanan tin canned good
maklumat information
malam night
malam ini tonight
malam tadi last night
malas lazy
mancis match
mandi shower
mangga lock
mangkuk bowl

manis sweet (taste)
masa time
masak sauteed (cooking method)
masalah problem
masam sour
masin salty
masjid mosque
masuk access; enter
mata eye
mata air panas hot spring
mata wang currency
matahari sun
mee noodles
meja table
mekanik mechanic
mel udara airmail
melampau overdone
melancong tour
melarang prohibit
melawat visit
melawat tempat-tempat sightseeing
Melayu Malay
meletak to park (car)
melihat see
melihat look
memadam delete
memakai wear
memanas heating
memanaskan warm
memandu drive
memandu melebihi had laju speeding
memanggang roast
memasak cook
memasukkan deposit; insert
membaiki fix; mend
membakar bake; burn
membalut wrap
membasuh wash
membatalkan cancel
membawa bring

membayar to be charged; to pay
membeli buy
membeli-belah shop; shopping
membenarkan allow; permit
memberhentikan sambungan disconnect (computer)
memberi give
membersihkan clean
memeluk hug
memepat trim
memeriksa check
memerlukan need
memesan order
meminda alter
mempamerkan display
memperbaiki repair
memperkenalkan introduce
mempreskripsikan prescribe
menaiki board
menaip type
menakjubkan magnificent
menambah fill up (food)
menangguh delay
menara tower
menari dance
menarik attractive; interesting; pull
mencabut extract (tooth)
mencadangkan recommend
mencetak print
mencium kiss
mencuri steal
mendaftar keluar check-out

mendaftar masuk check-in

mendail dial

mendapatkan have

menelan swallow

menelefon phone

menempah book; reserve

menerima accept; receive

mengadu complain

mengagumkan amazing

mengahwini marry

mengambil take (something)

mengandungi contain

menganyam weave

mengayuh basikal cycling

mengecap stamp (postage)

mengecas semula recharge

mengeja spell

mengeluarkan withdraw

mengemas pack

mengembalikan return (something)

mengembara tump-ang hitchhike

mengesahkan confirm

menggunakan use

menggunting cut (hair)

menghadiri attend

menghantar send

menghantar dengan kapal ship (mail)

menghantar faks fax

menghantar surat mail

menghantar teks text (send a message)

menghubungi notify

menginap stay

mengisi fill out (form)

mengisytiharkan declare

mengukir engrave

mengukur measure

mengulangi repeat

mengunci lock up

mengutip pick up (something)

menikmati enjoy

menjadi be

menjual sell

menolak to decline (credit card); to push

mentah raw

mentega butter

menterjemah translate

mentol lightbulb

menu dengan harga tetap fixed-price menu

menu kanak-kanak children's menu

menu minuman drink menu

menukar exchange; transfer (trains/ flights)

menukar change

menulis write

menunjukkan show

menyambung connect (internet)

menyebut pronounce

menyelam dive

menyertai join

menyeterika to iron (clothes)

menyewa hire; rent

menyewa kereta car hire

menyuap feed

merah red

merah jambu pink

meriah gay (happy)

merokok smoke

merompak to mug; to rob

merosakkan damage

message mesej segera instant

mesin basuh washing machine

mesin basuh pinggan mangkuk dishwasher

mesin layan diri vending machine

mesra kurang upaya handicapped-accessible

mesyuarat meeting

minat interested

minggu week

minggu yang lalu last week

minit minute

minta maaf sorry

minum drink

minuman beverage

minyak gas; oil

minyak diesel diesel

minyak tanpa plumbum unleaded (gas)

minyak wangi perfume

Misa mass (church service)

monorel monorail

motorbot motor boat

motorsikal motorcycle

muat fit (clothing)

muda young

muka face

muka surat pages (in a book)

mulut mouth

muntah vomit

murah cheap

mutiara pearl

muzik music

muzik klasik classical music

muzik rakyat folk music

muzium museum

N

nama name

nanas pineapple

nanti later

napkin napkin

nasi rice

negara country

nenek grandmother

nilai value

nombor number

nombor faks fax number

nombor lesen memandu driver's license number

nombor pengenalan diri personal identi-fication number (PIN)

nombor telefon phone number

nota notes

O

orang person

orang Amerika American

orang British British

orang Cina Chinese (person)

orang Ireland Irish

orang tua senior citizen

orang yang baru belajar beginner (skill level)

oren orange (color)
orkestra orchestra
otot muscle

P

padamkan turn off (lights)
padang field (sports)
padang golf golf course
pagi a.m./morning
paha thigh
pakai buang disposable
pakaian dalam underwear
pakaian clothing
pakar expert/specialist
pakar optik optician
pakar runding consultant
panas hot (temperature)
pancuran air fountain
panggil call
panggilan pagi wake-up call
panggilan pindah bayaran collect call
panggung wayang movie theater
pangsapuri apartment
panjang long
pantai beach
papan luncur air surfboard
papan panduan kedai store directory
paru-paru lung
pas masuk boarding pass
pasangkan turn on (lights)
pasar market

pasar malam night market
pasar raya mall; supermarket
pasport passport
pasukan team
patah broken (bone)
patung doll
payung umbrella
pecah break
pedas spicy
pegang hold
peguam lawyer
pejabat office
pejabat konsul consulate
pejabat maklumat pelancong tourist information office
pejabat pos post office
pejalan kaki pedestrian
pekak deaf
pelajar student
pelancong tourist
pelantar platform
pelayan lelaki waiter
pelayan perempuan waitress
pelik strange
pelocok plunger
peluncur air windsurfer
pemanas heater
pemandu guide (tourist)
pemanis tiruan artificial sweetener
pemarut grater
pembalut bandage
pembalut plastik plastic wrap
permbersih hampagas vacuum cleaner

pembuka botol bottle opener
pembuka selera appetizer; starter
pembuka tin can opener
pemetik api lighter
pemvaksinan vaccination
pencukur pakai buang disposable razor
pencuri thief
pendaftaran kenderaan vehicle registration
pendandan rambut hairstylist
pendek short
penerbangan flight
penerbangan antarabangsa international flight
penerbangan domestik domestic flight
pengajaran lesson (learnt a lesson)
penganggur unemployed
pengasuh bayi babysitter
pengeluaran withdrawal (bank)
pengetahuan knowledge
penghalau serangga insect repellent
pengimbas scanner
penginapan accommodation
pengukus steamer
pengurus manager
pengurutan massage
pengurutan sukan sports massage

pening dizzy
penisilin penicillin
penjual bunga florist
penjual daging butcher
penterjemahan interpreter
penting urgent
penuh full
penumpang passenger
penyahbau deodorant
penyakit anemia anemic
penyakit kelamin sexually transmitted disease
penyakit kencing manis diabetes
penyakit lelah asthma
penyaman udara air conditioning
penyapu broom
penyejuk beku freezer
penyeliaan supervision
penyembur rambut hairspray
penyepit chopsticks
penyerlah highlights (hair)
pepijat bug
perang brown
perak silver
perak tulen sterling silver
perapi conditioner (hair)
perbatuan mileage
percutian holiday
percutian vacation
perempuan female; woman
pergelangan tangan wrist

pergerakan mobility
pergi go (somewhere)
perhentian bas
  bus stop
periuk pot
perjalanan trip
perkakas utensil
perkhidmatan service
  (in a restaurant)
perkhidmatan penuh
  full-service
perlahan-lahan
  slowly
perlawanan bola
  sepak football game
perlawanan gusti
  wrestling
perlepasan departure
permainan game
permainan bola
  tampar volleyball
  game
perniagaan business
perpustakaan library
persiaran dengan
  bas bus tour
persidangan confer-
  ence
persimpangan
  intersection
pertama first
pertandingan golf
  golf tournament
pertandingan tinju
  boxing match
pertolongan help
pertukaran wang
  asing currency
  exchange
perut stomach
pesanan message
peta map
peta bandar town map
peta jalan road map
petang evening; p.m.

peti box
pintu keluar kece-
  masan emergency
  exit
pintu masuk entrance
pintu penghadang
  api fire door
pir pear
pisang banana
pisau knife
piuter pewter
poket pocket
pokok tree
polis police
porselin porcelain
pos post
poskad postcard
potongan rambut
  haircut
preskripsi prescription
Puan Madam/Mrs
puing ruins
pukul o'clock
puncak peak (of a
  mountain)
pundi kencing bladder
punggung buttocks
pusat center
putih white
puting pacifier

R

rabun blur; dim
rabun dekat long-
  sighted
rabun jauh short-
  sighted
racun poison
rahang jaw
rakan colleague;
  friend
ramalan forecast
rambut hair
rancangan plan
rantai chain

rantau region
rasa taste
rasa mual nauseous
ratu queen
rawatan kaki pedicure
rawatan muka facial
reaksi alah allergic
  reaction
rebus boil (cooking
  method)
rehat rest
rendah low
reneh poach (cooking
  method)
resit receipt
restoran restaurant
ribut petir thunder-
  storm
rogol rape
rokok cigarette
romantis romantic
rombongan excursion
rosak break down
roti bread
ruam rash
ruang makan dining
  room
rumah home; house
rumpai laut seaweed

S

sabun soap
saderi celery
sah laku valid
sains science
saiz size
saiz tambah plus size
sakit hurt; ill; pain;
  unwell
sakit dada chest pain
sakit jantung heart
  condition
sakit kepala headache
sakit kerongkong
  sore throat

sakit perut stom-
  achache
sakit perut akibat
  haid menstrual
  cramp
sakit telinga earache
salji snow
salun salon
saluran elektrik
  electric outlet
sama the same;
  identical
sama-sama you're
  welcome
sambilan part-time
sambungan connec-
  tion; extension
sampah rubbish; trash
sampul surat
  envelope
sana there
sandiwara play
  (theatre)
sangat really
sarapan pagi
  breakfast
sari kata subtitle
sarung kaki sock
sarung kamera
  camera case
satu one
saya I; me
sayur-sayuran
  vegetable
se- per
sebelah next to
sebelum before
sedang menari
  dancing
sedang menjalin
  hubungan attached
  (in a relationship)
sedap delicious
sederhana medium
  (size)

sedia ready
sedih sad
sedikit little; some
segar fresh
sehala one-way (ticket)
sehar per day
sejam per hour
sejuk cold; cool
sekali once
sekarang now
sekolah school
selada lettuce
selamat datang welcome
selamat jalan goodbye
selamat pagi good morning
selamat petang good evening
selamat tengah hari good afternoon
selaran matahari sunburn
selatan south
selekoh corner
selepas after
selimut blanket
selipar slippers
selsema cold (sickness)
seluar dalam briefs (clothing)
seluar panjang pants
seluar pendek shorts
semalam yesterday
semasa during
sembelit constipated
sementara temporary
seminggu per week
semula again
senang easy
senarai list
sendi joint (body part)

sendirian alone
sengat sting
serai lemongrass
serangan attack (on person)
servis bilik room service
sesat lost
sesiapa anyone
setengah half
seterusnya next
setiap minggu weekly
sewa kereta car rental
siapa who
sibuk busy
sijil certificate
sikat comb
siku elbow
sila please
simpan keep; save
simpan sejuk keep refrigerated
sini here
sirap syrup
sisa-sisa traces
sistem penerbangan airline
snek snacks
soalan question
sos sauce
sosej sausage
sotong squid
sotong kurita octopus
spesimen specimen
stesen station
stensen bawah tanah underground station
stesen keretapi train station
stesen minyak gas station
stik steak
strawberi strawberry
strok matahari sunstroke

suami husband
sudu spoon
sudu teh teaspoon
sudu ukuran measuring spoon
sudut pandangan viewpoint
suhu temperature
suka like
sukan sports
sungai river
sungguh really
sunyi quiet
sup soup
surat letter
surat berdaftar registered mail
surat khabar newspaper
susah difficult
susu milk
sut suit
sutera silk
syampu shampoo
syarikat company; firm

T

tahu know
tahun year
tajam sharp
tali leher tie (clothing)
tali pinggang belt
tali sawat penyampai conveyor belt
taman garden
taman hiburan amusement park
taman permainan playground
tamat end
tambahan extra
tambang fare (charge)
tampalan filling (tooth)

tandas restroom; toilet
tandatangan signature
tangan arm; hand
tangga stairs
tangga gerak elevator
tanggal take off (clothes)
tanjakan ramp
tanpa without
tanpa diawasi unattended
tanpa had unlimited
tanpa wayar wireless
tapak perkhemahan campsite
tarik nafas breathe deeply
tarikh date (calendar)
tarikh lupus expiration date
tasik lake
tauhu bean curd
tawar bland
tayar tire/tyre
teh tea
tekanan darah blood pressure
teksi taxi
telah berkahwin married
telah dicuri stolen
telah rosak damaged
telefon telephone
telefon awam pay phone
telefon mudah alih cell phone
televisyen TV
telinga ear
telur egg
teman lelaki boyfriend
teman wanita girlfriend
tembikai watermelon

tembikar pottery (goods)

tempahan reservation

tempat place

tempat berlabuh berth

tempat duduk seat

tempat duduk tepi lorong aisle seat

tempat meletak kereta parking lot

tempat menarik attraction (place)

tempat peranginan resort (holiday)

tempat pertempuran battleground

tempat tarikan utama main attraction

tempatan local

tendang kick

tengah hari afternoon; midday

tengah malam midnight

tenis tennis

tepat masa on-time

terakhir last

terang light (bright)

terbaik best

terbang; menerbang fly

terima kasih thank you

terjangkit infected

termasuk include

terseliuh sprain

tertutup closed

teruk terrible

terung ungu eggplant/ aubergine

terus straight

tiada not have

tiada apa-apa nothing

tiang pole; post

tiba arrive; reach

tidak makan daging vegetarian

tidak sedarkan diri unconscious

tidak no

tidur sleep

tikar mat; rug

tiket ticket

tiket elektronik e-ticket

tikus rat

timur east

tinggal live

tinggi high

tingkap window

tingkat storey

tisu tandas toilet paper

titik drop (medicine)

topi hat

topi keledar helmet

tradisional traditional

trak penarik tow truck

trek kuda horse track

troli cart; trolley

tua old (person)

tuala towel

tuala wanita sanitary napkin

tugu statue

tugu peringatan war memorial

tujuan purpose

tukang gunting rambut barber

tukul hammer

tulang bone

tulang belakang spine (body part)

tulang rusuk rib (body part)

tunggu wait

tuntutan bagasi baggage claim

turun get off (a train/ bus/subway)

tutup close (not open)

tingkat bawah ground floor

tiram oyster

tisu tissue

ubat medicine

ubat bius anesthesia

ubat gigi toothpaste

ubat tahan sakit painkiller

udang shrimp

udang galah lobster

udara air

ukiran carvings

ulang-alik round-trip

umbai usus appendix (body part)

umur age

ungu purple

universiti university

untuk for

utara north

W

waktu time

waktu melawat visiting hours

wang money

wang kertas currency note

wang pendahuluan cash advance

wang tunai cash

wanita lady; woman

wap air steam

warga Australia Australian

warga Kanada Canadian

warna color

wayang movie

Y

ya yes

yang the one which/ whom

yogurt yoghurt

Z

zaitun olive

zakar penis

zukini zucchini

INDEX

pocket guide

KUALA LUMPUR

Fourth Edition 2019

Editor: Sian Marsh
Author: Siew Lyn Wong and Paul Stafford
Head of DTP and Pre-Press: Rebeka Davies
Picture Editor: Tom Smyth
Cartography Update: Carte
Photography Credits: Apa Publications 17;
Corbis 20; Dreamstime 66, 68, 70; Fotolia
22; Getty Images 1; iStock 4ML, 5M; James
Tye/Apa Publications 5MC, 6L, 7, 7R, 11,
14, 26, 33, 50, 51, 52, 74, 79, 80, 84, 86, 99,
101; Jon Santa Cruz/Apa Publications 13,
24, 30, 38, 55, 57, 77, 81, 90; Nikt Wong/Apa
Publications 4TC, 5M, 6R, 19, 28, 34, 37, 39,
40, 43, 44, 46, 49, 59, 61, 63, 65, 73, 82, 83,
93, 95, 103; Shangri-La Hotels and Resorts
89; Shutterstock 4MC, 4TL, 5T, 5TC, 5MC
Cover Picture: Robert Harding

Distribution
UK, Ireland and Europe: Apa Publications
(UK) Ltd; sales@insightguides.com
United States and Canada: Ingram
Publisher Services; ips@ingramcontent.com
Australia and New Zealand: Woodslane;
info@woodslane.com.au
Southeast Asia: Apa Publications (SN) Pte;
singaporeoffice@insightguides.com
Worldwide: Apa Publications (UK) Ltd;
sales@insightguides.com

**Special Sales, Content Licensing
and CoPublishing**
Insight Guides can be purchased in bulk
quantities at discounted prices. We can
create special editions, personalised jackets
and corporate imprints tailored to your
needs. sales@insightguides.com;
www.insightguides.biz

All Rights Reserved
© 2019 Apa Digital (CH) AG and
Apa Publications (UK) Ltd

Printed in China by CTPS

No part of this book may be reproduced,
stored in a retrieval system or transmitted in
any form or means electronic, mechanical,
photocopying, recording or otherwise,
without prior written permission from Apa
Publications.

Contact us
Every effort has been made to provide
accurate information in this publication,
but changes are inevitable. The publisher
cannot be responsible for any resulting loss,
inconvenience or injury. We would appreciate
it if readers would call our attention to any
errors or outdated information. We also
welcome your suggestions; please contact
us at: berlitz@apaguide.com
www.insightguides.com/berlitz

Berlitz Trademark Reg. U.S. Patent Office
and other countries. Marca Registrada.
Used under licence from the Berlitz
Investment Corporation

Kuala Lumpur Rail Transit

1 KTM Seremban Line
2 KTM Port Klang Line
3 LRT Ampang Line
4 LRT Sri Petaling Line
5 LRT Kelana Jaya Line
6 KLIA Ekspres Line
7 KLIA Transit Line
8 KL Monorail Line
9 MRT Sungai Buloh - Kajang Line
10 Skypark Link
○ Interchange station
Interchange station within walking distance

Berlitz®

speaking your language

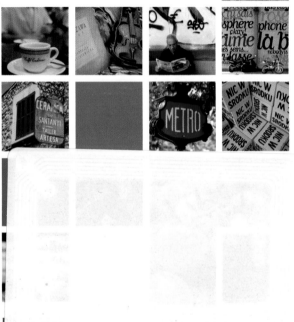

phrase book & CD

Available in: Arabic, Brazilian Portuguese*, Burmese*, Cantonese Chinese, Croatian, Czech*, Danish*, Dutch, English, Filipino, Finnish*, French, German, Greek, Hebrew*, Hindi*, Hungarian*, Indonesian, Italian, Japanese, Korean, Latin American Spanish, Malay, Mandarin Chinese, Mexican Spanish, Norwegian, Polish, Portuguese, Romanian*, Russian, Spanish, Swedish, Thai, Turkish, Vietnamese
*Book only

www.berlitzpublishing.com